LORD, TEACH ME TO PRAY for kids

KAY ARTHUR
JANNA ARNDT

HARVEST HOUSE PUBLISHERS
EUGENE, OREGON

All Scripture quotations are taken from the New American Standard Bible®, © 1960, 1962, 1963, 1968, 1971, 1972, 1973, 1975, 1977, 1995 by The Lockman Foundation. Used by permission.

DISCOVER FOR YOURSELF is a registered trademark of The Hawkins Children's LLC. Harvest House Publishers, Inc., is the exclusive licensee of the federally registered trademark DISCOVER 4 YOURSELF.

Cover & interior illustrations by Steve Bjorkman Studio, Irvine, California

Cover by Left Coast Design, Portland, Oregon

SUSTAINABLE FORESTRY INITIATIVE
Label applies to the text stock

Certified Sourcing
www.sfiprogram.org
SFI-00341

Discover 4 Yourself® Inductive Bible Studies for Kids

LORD, TEACH ME TO PRAY FOR KIDS

Copyright © 2002 by Precept Ministries International
Published by Harvest House Publishers
Eugene, Oregon 97402
www.harvesthousepublishers.com

ISBN 978-0-7369-0666-1

Printed in the United States of America.

12 13 14 15 16 17 18 19 / ML-KB / 19 18 17 16 15 14 13 12

To five precious women who faithfully pray for me—
You are among my greatest blessings:

My mom, Ramona Vickery
My sister, Rhonda Usry,
And my sisters in Christ,
Kathy Dean,
Leslie Murphree, and
Sherry Lundy

We have shared both our greatest joys and our deepest sorrows.
Our loving Father has used it all for our good and bound us together
through the awesome privilege of coming to Him in prayer.
I am so grateful for each one of you.
I love you,
Janna

I thank my God in all my remembrance of you,
always offering prayer with joy in my every prayer for you all….
For I am confident of this very thing, that He who began a good work in
you will perfect it until the day of Christ Jesus.

Philippians 1:3-4,6

Hey, parents, did you know that Kay has also written a book on prayer for adults? It's called **Lord, Teach Me to Pray in 28 Days.** *In it Kay provides intensely practical insights to help you know how to pray, and what to expect when you pray.*

Thankfully, Jesus gave His disciples the perfect pattern for meaningful prayer. It is refreshingly simple and exceedingly powerful, and it can begin to transform the way you pray (and live) today!

For more information, contact Precept Ministries International at 800-763-8280 or visit Precept's website at www.precept.org.

CONTENTS

Learning to Pray—
A Bible Study You Can Do!

At ease, soldier. It's good to have you with us. Welcome to Camp MacHaven, the training facility for God's Special Forces. What is God's Special Forces? It's an elite team made up of guys and girls like you who want to know God (the Commander in Chief) and have a special relationship with Him.

To become a part of God's A team, you will spend the next 28 days on God's "Q" course, being trained as a communications specialist and learning how to pray. It's very important to know how to pray God's way because prayer is our direct line of communication with the Commander in Chief.

During "Q" course training, you will study God's training manual, the Bible, the source of all truth, through a special method called inductive Bible study. *Inductive* means you go straight to the Bible *yourself* to discover what it means, instead of depending on what someone else says it means.

So, soldier, are you up to the challenge of God's "Q" course? Do you want to be a member of God's A team, a part of His Special Forces? If so, you must be willing to spend time with God each day so that you can give Him your all and follow His orders.

Great! Head to the barracks to unpack your gear. Training begins at 0600 hours. See you there!

Equipment You'll Need
▼

New American Standard Bible (Updated Edition)—or preferably, the New Inductive Study Bible (NISB)

Pen or Pencil

Colored Pencils

Index Cards

A Dictionary

This Workbook

1

A SPECIAL MISSION— OPERATION PRAYER

Hit the deck! Up and at 'em soldier! Your first assignment at Camp MacHaven is to attend the captain's briefing on communication for our special mission, Operation Prayer. So hit the showers. Grab those training manuals and get some chow from the mess hall. You need to be at the team's command center by 0700 hours.

A COMMUNICATION BRIEFING

Welcome to Camp MacHaven, soldiers. To become a communications specialist for God's A team, you need to understand what communication is and why it is important.

Communication is the way we share our thoughts and ideas. We can communicate by writing letters, sending e-mails, talking in person, and calling on the telephone. Soldiers use these methods, but they also communicate by sending and receiving radio transmissions, and sometimes by using secret codes.

Communication is vital to soldiers. It can be critical to their survival, especially in war. Communication is the way soldiers get their orders and stay in touch with their commander so they will know when they should move in or pull out. It is the way they send for help, order their supplies, as well as find out who their enemy is and what he's up to.

Communication is the key to all of our relationships, whether parent to child, friend to friend, or commander to soldier. What would happen if you didn't spend time talking with and listening to your best friend? Would you stay best friends? No. We develop friendships little bit by little bit as we spend time talking and listening to each other. It's the way we get to know one another and stay close.

That's why your training time on God's "Q" course will be spent learning how to pray. To have a relationship with our Commander in Chief, we have to spend time talking with and getting to know Him. And that's what prayer is: talking with and listening to God. God loves you and wants to be close to you. He created you to have a relationship with Him.

Prayer is a special privilege that God has given us so that we can talk with Him anytime, anywhere, about anything. Just think: You have direct access to the Commander in Chief, the Ruler of the universe!!

Isn't that awesome? It's kind of like having the private phone number of the president of the United States and being able to call him anytime, day or night, knowing he will be there ready to listen.

Prayer is an exciting adventure, but it isn't something we know how to do automatically. Just like soldiers train and practice every day to develop their skills, prayer takes training and practice. That's what we will do on God's "Q" course. First, we will develop our prayer know-how by studying our training manual (the Bible), and then we will practice, practice, practice by spending time communicating with our Commander in Chief. As God's Special Forces, we want to "be all we can be." We want our relationship with our Commander in Chief to be the very best!

Now that you have completed your communications briefing, let's get started. But first things first. WHAT does a soldier need to do before he begins his mission? The first thing a soldier needs to do is to check in with his commander. So grab your SATCOM (your satellite communications radio) and bow before God's throne. Ask your Commander in Chief to help you get to know Him and to teach you how to pray.

Good work, soldier! We're good to go. Now let's take a look at our training manual. Did you know that the Bible, our training manual, is another way that our Commander in Chief communicates with us? Read 1 John 5:14-15 printed out below:

> *This is the confidence which we have before Him, that, if we ask anything according to His will, He hears us. And if we know that He hears us in whatever we ask, we know that we have the requests which we have asked from Him.*

Now go back and read those verses again and mark the key words. What are key words? Key words are words that pop up more than once. They are called key words because they help unlock the meaning of the chapter or book that you are studying and give you clues about what is most important in a passage of Scripture.

- Key words are usually used over and over again.
- Key words are important.
- Key words are used by the writer for a reason.

Once you discover a key word, you need to mark it in a special way using a special color or symbol so that you can immediately spot it in the Scripture passage. Don't forget to mark any pronouns that go with the key words, too! WHAT are pronouns? Check out our map on the next page.

PRONOUNS

Pronouns are words that take the place of nouns. A noun is a person, place, or thing. A pronoun stands in for a noun! Here's an example: "Special Force soldiers must pass the obstacle course. They have to be able to jump off walls, climb ropes, and crawl through underground pipes to be prepared for any circumstance." The word *they* is a pronoun because it takes the place of *Special Force soldiers* in the second sentence. It is another word we use to refer to the soldiers.

Watch for these other pronouns when you are marking people:

I	you	he	she
me	yours	him	her
mine		his	hers
we	it	they	
our	its	them	
ours		their	

Now that you know what key words and pronouns are, go back to 1 John 5:14-15 on page 9 and mark:

God (the *He* and *Him* in these verses) (draw a purple triangle and color it yellow)

ask (color it blue)   hears (draw a green ear)

According to 1 John 5:14-15, WHAT is the confidence we have before God?

He hears us and listions to our prayrs

He will anser them now matter what

WHEN God hears us, will He give us our requests? _Yes! if this will_

Is it God's will that we know how to pray? _YES!_

Yes. God wants a relationship with us. All we need to do is ask. These verses show us that we can be confident that God will hear us if we come to Him and ask according to His will.

Way to go, soldier! As we wrap up our first assignment, write a brief message to the Commander in Chief on the lines below. Just use your own words and keep it simple. God wants us to be honest and share our heart with Him. Learning to pray is not about our performance; it's about having a close and loving relationship with God.

Begin by thanking Him for the awesome privilege of having direct access to Him. Thank Him for His promise in 1 John 5:14-15 that He will hear us and give us what we ask for, if we ask according to His will. Thank Him for giving us His Word. Tell Him that you know it's His will that you learn how to pray, that you want to get to know Him and be a part of His Special Forces.

Dear Lord thank you for

such a wonderful day and

pleese let me have fun this

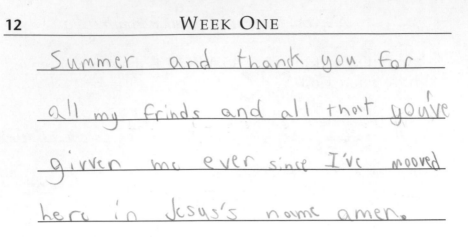

Summer and thank you for all my frinds and all that you've givven me ever since I've mooved here in Jesus's name amen.

You did it, soldier—mission complete!

TRAINING EXERCISES

"Okay, soldiers, it's time to hit the training area," stated Captain Bryant as we finished our morning exercises. "It is very important for a GSF (God's Special Forces) soldier to know how to collect and evaluate information. Field training will teach you how to develop this very important skill."

First, we will observe one of God's prayer warriors, and then we will gather information by asking questions. GSF soldiers need to develop good observation skills. They need to know how to ask the 5 W's and an H. WHAT are the 5 W's and an H? They are the WHO, WHAT, WHERE, WHEN, WHY, and HOW questions.

    1. Asking WHO helps you find out:

WHO wrote this?

To WHOM was it written?

WHOM are we reading about?

WHO said this or did that?

2. WHAT helps you understand:

WHAT is the author talking about?

WHAT are the main things that happen?

3. WHERE helps you learn:

WHERE did something happen?

WHERE did they go?

WHERE was this said?

When we discover a "WHERE" we double-underline the "WHERE" in green.

4. WHEN tells us about time. We mark it with a green clock like this: 🕐

WHEN tells us:

WHEN did this event happen or WHEN will it happen?

WHEN did the main characters do something? It helps us to follow the order of events. Timing (knowing when) is critical for soldiers. They have to be able to coordinate their missions.

5. WHY asks questions like:

WHY did he say that?   WHY did this happen?

WHY did they go there?

6. HOW lets you figure out things like:

HOW is something to be done?

HOW did people know something had happened?

Now that you have your orders, what do you need to do first? Pray! You've got it down. Ask the Commander in Chief to guide you as you hit the training area. Then move out, soldier. Read James 5:16-18 printed out below and ask the 5 W's and an H:

> **16** Therefore, confess your sins to one another, and pray for one another so that you may be healed. The effective prayer of a righteous man can accomplish much. **17** Elijah was a man with a nature like ours, and he prayed earnestly that it would not rain, and it did not rain on the earth for three years and six months. **18** Then he prayed again, and the sky poured rain and the earth produced its fruit.

James 5:16 WHAT kind of prayer can accomplish much and from WHAT kind of man?

the __e f fctive__ prayer of a __righteous__ man

A righteous man is a person who has been made right with God. It is someone who realizes that he is a sinner and has confessed his sins. He has asked Jesus to be his Savior and now has a right relationship with God. He wants to do what God says is right in His Word.

James 5:17 WHO prayed that it would not rain?

Elijah

James 5:17 WHAT kind of man was he?

A righteous man.

That means that Elijah was just an ordinary guy like you and me.

James 5:17 HOW did he pray?

<u>effctively</u>

Being earnest means that he was sincere. He prayed genuinely, honestly, eagerly, with deep feelings. Elijah prayed with a purpose.

James 5:17 WHAT did he pray for?

<u>no rain</u>

James 5:17 WHAT was the result of his prayer? WHAT happened?

<u>he praid for no rain so there was non for 3 and a 1/2 years.</u>

James 5:18 WHAT happened in this verse?

<u>then he prayd for rain and it did</u>

Did God answer Elijah's prayers? <u>Yes</u>

Are you amazed that an ordinary guy was able to pray the heavens shut and then pray them back open? HOW did Elijah, who was just an ordinary guy, do something so extraordinary? We know he prayed earnestly. HOW did Elijah know what to pray for?

Let's gather more information from your training manual by doing some cross-referencing. WHAT is cross-referencing? Cross-referencing is where we compare Scripture with

Scripture by going to other passages in the Bible. This is a very important Bible study tool to help us search out the meaning of Scripture because we know that Scripture never contradicts Scripture.

Look up and read 1 Kings 17:1.

WHOM did Elijah tell it would not rain?

AHAB

Look up and read 1 Kings 16:30-31.

1 Kings 16:30 WHAT kind of king was Ahab?

I bad Dude!!

1 Kings 16:31 WHOM did Ahab serve and worship?

BAAL

Wow! Can you believe that Elijah had the courage to tell evil King Ahab that it wouldn't rain? HOW did Elijah know?

Look up and read Deuteronomy 11:13-17.

Deuteronomy 11:13-14 WHAT would God give to those who obeyed His commandments?

rain good crops

Deuteronomy 11:16-17 WHAT would happen if they turned away and served other gods? WHAT would God take away?

rain, and the crops wold Dye then the people wold die

1 Kings 16:31 Was King Ahab serving and worshiping other gods? Yes

Elijah had the confidence to tell King Ahab it wouldn't rain because he knew what God had told Moses. Elijah knew God's Word.

Elijah was just an ordinary guy who was able to see God do the extraordinary because he knew how to pray. Can you accomplish the extraordinary, like Elijah did, with your prayers? Yes! Knowing God and His Word will show you how to pray with extraordinary results just like Elijah.

Before you leave the field, practice what you have learned. Ask God to teach you how to pray like Elijah so that you can be effective and accomplish much.

> *Father, I want to learn how to pray like Elijah. Please teach me how to pray as I study Your Word and put my faith and my trust in You. Teach me how to pray the prayer of a righteous man that accomplishes much. I know it's Your will, so I am asking for You to show me how. Thank You for hearing my prayer, in the name of Your Son, Jesus Christ, who loves me and died for me. Amen.*

Now draw a picture in the box below of Elijah earnestly praying to God. Ask for God's help and encouragment as you train to be one of His Special Forces.

PRAYER TRAINING WITH THE COMMUNICATIONS EXPERT

Fall in, soldiers. Yesterday we developed our observation skills as we learned how to ask questions and gather information about one of God's prayer warriors, Elijah.

Today we need to continue working on these observation exercises as we get special prayer training from our communications expert. WHO is our communications expert? You'll find out. So grab your SATCOM and check in with the Commander in Chief.

Then head to your Observation Worksheets. Observation Worksheets are pages from your training manual. They have the Bible text printed out for you to use in your field exercises. So turn to page 149 and read your Observation Worksheet on Luke 11:1-10 to meet our expert on prayer. Then gather the information by asking the 5 W's and an H.

Luke 11:1 WHO was praying? __Jesus__

WHAT did one of His disciples ask Him to do?

__Teach him to pray__

Are you surprised that Jesus' disciples asked for help in learning how to pray? After all, they were disciples. Jesus had chosen them to follow Him. But think how they must have felt as they walked with Jesus and watched His very powerful prayers. They probably thought they could never pray like Him. But instead of giving up, they went to the communications expert and asked Him to teach them. What an encouragement! Since Jesus taught the disciples how to pray, then we know that prayer is a skill that we can learn, too.

Luke 11:5-8 WHAT illustration does Jesus use to teach the disciples about prayer?

A friend asks for help

Luke 11:8 WHY does he get up and give his friend what he needs?

becase he is persistant

Luke 11:9-10 HOW will it be given to you?

In the way your looking for you

HOW will you find?

by Seeking

HOW will it be opened?

by Knocking

Go back to your Observation Worksheet on page 149 and circle these three verbs in Luke 11:9 in blue.

WHAT do we learn about prayer from this illustration? Luke 11:8 HOW did the friend get him out of the bed?

Because of his Persistance

Prayer requires persistence. Persistence is not giving up. The three verbs we just looked at—*ask, seek,* and *knock*—are all in the present tense in the Greek.

If you have done *How to Study Your Bible for Kids,* then you may remember that a Greek verb in the present tense means it is a continuous action. That means it keeps on happening. We are not to just ask, seek, and knock once, but we are to keep on doing it.

Why do you think Jesus tells us to keep on asking, seeking, and knocking? Maybe it's because, like a soldier, we need to stay in constant communication with our Commander in Chief. We need to learn how to be persistent. God wants soldiers who don't give up even when the going gets tough. Practice being persistent by telling God that you want to know how to pray, that you are going to keep asking, seeking, and knocking.

> *Father, thank You for communicating with me through Your Word. I learned in Luke 11:1-10 that Jesus taught His disciples how to pray. Please teach me, too. I ask for Your help. I am seeking and knocking. Please hear me and answer my prayer. I want to be a member of Your A team. I will keep on asking. I want to depend on You. I want to be persistent in prayer. Thank You for hearing me and answering. I love You. In Jesus' name. Amen.*

DISCOVERING A SPECIAL CODE

Good morning, soldier. You have a very tough training schedule ahead of you today. First you need to do what? That's right—grab your SATCOM and get your orders from the Commander in Chief.

Now that you have checked in, you are ready to do some field training with our communications expert to develop those communications skills. Once field training is complete, you will be off to the obstacle course to do some wall climbing and jumping.

Then you need to pack those rucksacks with your MREs (meals ready to eat). You also need plenty of water, your sleeping gear, and navigation equipment for your cross-country land navigation.

So are you ready? Good. Grab some chow and let's head over to the training area. We need to pick up where we left off yesterday. Let's find out what our communications expert taught His disciples about prayer.

Turn to your Observation Worksheet on page 149 and read Luke 11:1-4.

> Luke 11:2 HOW did Jesus respond to the disciples' request? WHAT did Jesus say to them?

<u>And he said to them when you pray say</u>
<u>father Howled be your name your kengdom</u> come.

These verses in Luke 11:2-4 are known as "the Lord's Prayer." Do you think that when Jesus gave these verses and told His disciples "when you pray, say:" that He wanted the disciples to pray by just repeating these words over and over? ____ Yes ✓ No

Now let's look at a cross-reference for the Lord's Prayer in Matthew 6. As we do, we need to look at context. WHAT is context? Context is the setting in which something is found. It is very important in Bible study. Context is a combination of two words: *con*, which means "with," and text, which means "what is written."

So when you look for context in the Bible, you look at the verses and chapters surrounding the passage you are studying, as well as see how it fits into the whole Bible.

Since Matthew 6 (our cross-reference passage) begins with someone speaking and it doesn't tell us who this person is, we need to look at the verses that come before Matthew 6 to find out who is speaking.

Context also includes:

- The place something happens. (This is geographical context, such as knowing where Jesus lived. Did Jesus live in Israel or the United States?)

- The time in history an event happens. (This is historical context, such as the time before Jesus' birth, during His life, or after His death and resurrection.)

- The customs of a group of people. (This is cultural context. For instance, did Jesus wear a tunic, or did He wear blue jeans?)

Now that we know what context is, look up the passage that comes before our cross-reference passage on Matthew 6.

Look up and read Matthew 5:1-2.

Matthew 5:1-2 WHO is teaching? __Jesus__

Now turn to your Observation Worksheet on Matthew 6 on page 153. Since we have looked at the passage in Matthew 5 and discovered that Jesus was teaching on the mountain, do we know who is speaking in Matthew 6:1? Yes. Context shows us that Matthew 6 is a continuation of Jesus' teaching on the mountain in Matthew 5.

Read Matthew 6:7-15.

Matthew 6:7 WHAT does Jesus tell them not to do when they pray?

__Repeat__

So does that sound like Jesus wanted them to just memorize "the Lord's Prayer" and repeat it back to God? __no__

No. First, Jesus says not to use meaningless repetition. That means that Jesus doesn't want them to repeat words that have no meaning to them. In verse 9 He tells them to "pray, then, in this way." Jesus doesn't want them to pray by just repeating the Lord's Prayer; instead, He is teaching them a way to pray. Remember, they did not have books. They only had scrolls, which were written by hand and very expensive to own.

So Jesus uses the Lord's Prayer to model prayer for them. The Lord's Prayer is a collection of seven brief sentences that cover different topics to pray about. It is an outline that covers every detail of prayer. This was also the method that the rabbis used for teaching. Jesus gave the Lord's Prayer to be like a special code that would not only be a teaching guide, but it would also help the disciples remember how to pray since they didn't have a Bible of their own.

The rest of our training time in God's "Q" course will be spent learning how to pray by using this special method that Jesus, our communications expert, taught His disciples. Are you willing to set aside a special time every day to meet with God and focus on your relationship with Him? Then you have what it takes to complete God's "Q" course and earn your GSF beret.

First, we will memorize this code—not so we can repeat it over and over, word by word, as a prayer to God, but so we can learn what God wants us to pray about. Once we know the code, we will decipher it by taking each one of the seven sentences and looking at them one at a time to discover what subject each sentence covers.

Then we will have the know-how to communicate with our Commander in Chief. Doesn't that sound awesome? You are going to develop the skills to become a communications specialist and start a very exciting lifetime adventure with the Ruler of the universe!

Let's get started. Write out Matthew 6:9-13 on the lines below:

Pray, then in this way:

Our father in heaven, Hollowed be

your kingdom come your will be done onearth as it is in heave give us this day our daily bread and forgive us our debts as we forgive our debtors lead us not into temptation but deliver us from evil for Thinds the power and the glory forever amen.

Now that you have the code, soldier, get to work. Practice drilling this code by saying it aloud three times in a row, three times each day—morning, noon, and night—until you have it down. All right! Your Commander is soooooo proud of your drill skills!

DECIPHERING THE CODE

You did a terrific job in the field on your land navigation exercises! As we get started on Phase II of our "Q" course training, we will continue to develop our communications skills.

GSF soldiers are trained to use not only high-tech radios, advanced computer networking, and encryption techniques (*encryption* means "to put in a secret code") but also basic Morse code. They are trained and prepared for all situations since high-tech communications gear can fail due to batteries that run down and satellites that can be disabled.

So grab those training manuals, and don't forget to check in with the Commander in Chief. Then head over to the communications center to study Jesus' special code (the Lord's Prayer). We need to look at each one of these seven sentences to decipher the special code and discover what subject is being taught in this model on prayer.

Then we can give each sentence a title to help us remember each subject as we learn how to pray. A title is a very brief description that describes the main thing the sentence is about.

Take a look at the first sentence in Matthew 6:9-13. "Pray, then, in this way: 'Our Father who is in heaven, hallowed be Your name.'"

> WHAT do you think the main subject is in this sentence? Write out a short title that describes the main subject.
>
> _Holley is your name._

Now take a look at the next sentence: "Your kingdom come."

Give the second sentence a title.

> _Gods kingdom_

"Your will be done, on earth as it is in heaven."

Title this sentence.

Every thing to be don on Earth
like it is in heaven

"Give us this day our daily bread."

Title this sentence.

pervied our needs

"And forgive us our debts, as we also have forgiven our debtors."

Title this sentence.

forgive us as we forgive others

"And do not lead us into temptation, but deliver us from evil."

Write out your title for this sentence.

lead us not into evel

"For Yours is the kingdom and the power and the glory forever. Amen."

Title this last sentence in the Lord's Prayer.

For God is the power and the
Glory forever omen

Now let's see how you did, soldier. Let's check your answers by comparing them to the "Q" course manual on the Lord's Prayer. As you look under each sentence of the Lord's Prayer on page 28, the "Q" course manual gives you the main subject for that sentence in Morse code.

Morse code was invented as a way to send messages over the telegraph very quickly using a code of dots (.) and dashes (_). These patterns of dots and dashes each represent a letter of the alphabet or a number.

Decode the main subject for each sentence of the Lord's Prayer in the "Q" course manual on page 28 by looking at the Morse Code Answer Key below and writing the letter that is represented by the dots and dashes on the blanks underneath the code in your manual.

Manual for "Q" Course

	Morse Code Answer Key	
A . _	B _ . . .	C _ . _ .
D _ . .	E .	F . . _ .
G _ _ .	H	I . .
J . _ _ _	K _ . _	L . _ . .
M _ _	N _ .	O _ _ _
P . _ _ .	Q _ _ . _	R . _ .
S . . .	T _	U . . _
V . . . _	W . _ _	X _ . . _
Y _ . _ _	Z _ _ . .	1 . _ _ _ _
2 . . _ _ _	3 . . . _ _	4 . . . . _
5	6 _	7 _ _ . . .
8 _ _ _ . .	9 _ _ _ _ .	0 _ _ _ _ _

We did the first few letters in the first sentence for you.
Pray, then, in this way:

"Our Father who is in heaven, hallowed be Your name."

W O R __ __ __ . __ __ __ . . . . __ __ __ . . . __ __ __

W O R S h i p

"Your kingdom come."

A L L E G I A N C E

"Your will be done, on earth as it is in heaven."

S u B M I S S I O N

"Give us this day our daily bread."

P E T I T I O N   and

I N T E R P E S S I O N

"And forgive us our debts, as we also have forgiven our debtors."

C O N F E S S I O N   and

F O R G i v e n e s s

"And do not lead us into temptation, but deliver us from evil."

D E L I V E R A N C E

"For Yours is the kingdom and the power and the glory forever. Amen."

W O R S H I P

Awesome! You are on your way to becoming a communications specialist. Don't worry if the words in your titles aren't exactly like the ones you decoded in our training manual. That doesn't mean that you have the wrong answers. You just need to make sure that your title covers the same subject as ours, even though you may have used different words to describe it.

WHY don't you turn to page 153 to your Observation Worksheet on Matthew 6 and write each title next to the sentence it goes with in the Lord's Prayer?

Now let's run through your drills by practicing the Lord's Prayer. As you say each sentence aloud, pause and add the main topic. As you say, "Our Father who is in heaven, hallowed be Your name," stop and say aloud, "This means worship." Then go to the next sentence and continue to do the same thing all the way through the Lord's Prayer. Drilling this skill every day will help you remember Jesus' code and what it means so that you can know exactly how to pray.

JUST FOR FUN

Okay, soldiers, now that you have those drills down, how would you like to have fun by learning how to transmit a message using Morse code?

First you need a friend, brother, sister, or parent to be your partner for you to transmit your secret message to. Then you need to choose if you want to flash your message with flashlights or use sound with a buzzer or bell.

Now if you are using a buzzer or a bell, look at your Morse Code Answer Key (your partner will need a copy of the answer key, too), and use a short burst of sound to represent the dot, and a longer sound (equal to the sound of three dot lengths) to represent each dash. You also need to pause between letters (your pause should be about three dot lengths long).

If you want to use a flashlight to send your message, you need to flash your flashlight briefly on and off to represent the dots. Leave the flashlight on longer (equal three short flashes) to represent the dashes.

You'll have to go slowly since you are just learning and will need time to check your answer key to figure out the letters. You may even want to use paper and a pencil to write down the dots and dashes as they are flashed and then check your code for the correct letter.

Also, instead of flashing long words, you might want to make up your own secret code to use as an abbreviation. For an example, to say, "I need help," you would flash the signals for SOS (which is a code that is abbreviated), instead of flashing each word in "I need help."

Think of several messages with your friend, and then give each message a short abbreviation, or use your topics for prayer. Then grab your transmitter (your flashlight or buzzer) and have fun sending your secret messages.

BACK TO THE TRAINING AREA

You did a fantastic job deciphering Jesus' code at the communications center yesterday. Now that we have uncovered all the main subjects that show us what we need to pray about, we need to grab our gear and head back to the training area. Did you remember to check in with the Commander in Chief?

Then we're good to go. Our first training exercise will be to take a closer look at the first sentence in the Lord's Prayer.

"Pray, then, in this way: 'Our Father who is in heaven, hallowed be Your name.'"

WHY do you think Jesus began with this sentence?
WHAT is prayer?

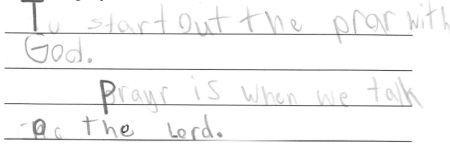

To start out the prar with God.

Prayr is when we talk to the Lord.

WHERE is God?

In heaven

WHAT is God like? WHAT is He called in this sentence?

Our father in heaven

True prayer is spiritual fellowship with the Father, not with an untouchable, far-off God. Prayer is directed to our Father. He loves us. He cares about us and wants us to spend time talking to Him, just as a child talks to his father. Isn't it amazing that we get to call the Ruler of the universe *Father?*

Now read Hebrews 11:6 printed out below:

And without faith it is impossible to please Him,
for he who comes to God must believe that He is and
that He is a rewarder of those who seek Him.

Looking at this passage in Hebrews 11:6, WHAT is necessary to please God?

Faith

WHAT is faith? Look up Hebrews 11:1 in your training manual (your Bible) and write out what faith is.

Confidence that we hope life for will actuly happen

Looking back at Hebrews 11:6, WHAT do we have to do?

We haft to belive God

Hebrews 11:6 WHAT do we have to believe?

That God is Real

Faith is believing God. It means that even though we haven't seen Him, we are convinced, we have confidence that God is there, that He is WHO He says He is, that He is the Rewarder, and that He will do what He says in the Bible.

So WHAT have we learned in our training exercise today?

1. We need to c _o m e_ to God.

2. HOW do we come? WHAT do we have to have?

   f _a i t n_

3. WHO is God? WHAT is He like?

   our _father_

Do you see how the foundation of prayer is faith in God? We have to believe God before we can come to Him. Now that we know how to come to God, we need to know WHAT our Father is like. To find this out, we need to keep studying His Word. God reveals Himself to us in the Bible, so the more we read and study the Bible, the more we will know and understand WHO God is. We have already seen that Elijah was able to pray the heavens open and shut because he knew how great God is.

Let's take a look at James 1:17 printed out below:

Every good thing given and every perfect gift is from above, coming down from the Father of lights, with whom there is no variation or shifting shadow.

WHAT comes from the Father of lights?

Every good thing given

WHAT does it say about the Father of lights?

"with whom there is _no_ _variation_ or _Shifting shadow_ "

That means that the Father of lights never changes. God is always the same in His nature, His character, and His will. He is the same yesterday, today, and tomorrow.

Did you know that God was the Giver of every perfect gift, and that He never changes? You can trust and depend on God because He doesn't change His mind or WHO He is.

As you march back to the barracks, why don't you spend some time thinking about what you learned about coming to God? Then praise Him for being faithful and trustworthy, the Giver of every good and perfect gift. Fantastic! And don't forget to practice your drills for our special code on prayer three times today!

TRAINING EXERCISES WITH THE COMMANDER OF JUDAH

Rise and shine, soldiers! Check in with the Commander in Chief, pack your rucksacks, and don't forget your ERGO drink full of vitamins and minerals and your HOOAH! bar to give you all the nutrition and energy you need to keep your mind alert and delay fatigue as you march back into the field.

Today we need to work on our training exercises to discover what the commander of Judah, a king named Jehoshaphat, knew about God. Turn to page 156 of your Observation Worksheets and read 2 Chronicles 20:1-30.

2 Chronicles 20:1 WHAT did the sons of Moab, the sons of Ammon, and some of the Meunites come to do to Jehoshaphat?

To come to war

2 Chronicles 20:3 HOW did Jehoshaphat feel?

Afraid

WHAT did Jehoshaphat do?

he gatherd help aginst the Lord

2 Chronicles 20:4 WHAT did Judah do?

he gatherd help angenst the Lord

2 Chronicles 20:6 HOW did Jehoshaphat begin his prayer?

Oh Lord, the God of heavens

Did you see this in the Lord's Prayer? Yes

HOW does Jehoshaphat worship God? Make a list of HOW he describes God in verses 6-12:

Verse 6: God of our fathers

God in the heavens

Ruler over all the kingdoms of the nations

Power and mite are in Your hand.

No one can stand against You.

Verse 7: God drive out the inhabitants of this land.

God is it to the descendants of Abraham.

God is Abraham's faith forever.

Verse 9: When we cry to God in distress, He will

hear and forgive us.

Verse 12: God is the jesus.

Our eyes are on You.

Wow! WHAT a prayer of praise. Did God answer? Look at what God says in verses 15-17:

Verse 15: The powers is not yours but God's.

Verse 17: Stand and see the ___people___ of the

Lord on your behalf. The Lord is ___with___ you.

2 Chronicles 20:18 WHAT happens?

___Jehowis prays.___

2 Chronicles 20:20 WHAT does Jehoshaphat tell them?

"Put your ___faith___ in the ___Lord___ your God."

"Put your ___trust___ in His prophets and ___Him___."

2 Chronicles 20:21 WHAT did they say as they went out before the army?

"Give ___Thank___ to the LORD, for His

___power___ is ___forever___."

2 Chronicles 20:23-27 WHAT happened? Were they successful? Did they defeat their enemies? ___Yes___

Isn't that amazing? Jehoshaphat knew God. He had faith. He knew how to come to God and ask for His help when he was afraid. First Jehoshaphat praised God for who He is, then he asked God for His help. He reminded God that they were powerless and needed Him.

HOW would you stand if you were facing an enemy? Would you know what to do? Do you know God? Would you put your trust in Him?

If you don't think you know God well enough, don't give up. Go to Him and tell Him that you want to know Him better. Then keep doing what you are doing right now—keep studying His Word.

Fantastic training exercise—keep up the good work! Before you chow down on that HOOAH! bar and ERGO drink, take a moment and think about something you learned about God today, such as: He is the Ruler, power and might are in His hand. Then go to the Father and get some prayer practice in. Praise God for what you know about Him!

2

WORSHIP, ALLEGIANCE, AND SUBMISSION TO THE COMMANDER IN CHIEF

Good morning, soldiers. You have worked hard to complete the first week of "Q" course training to become a GSF soldier. Look at all the territory you covered as you hit the field in Phase I using your training manuals to gather information and develop your observation skills.

As you moved into Phase II, you decoded our communications expert's prayer and began your training on how to approach the Commander in Chief.

This week we will continue to be equipped to approach our Commander in Chief, and to prepare for times of crisis when our Commander sends us downrange. We also need to know how to keep a logbook of all our communications to strengthen our faith, and to discover exactly what it takes to give our allegiance to our Commander's kingdom. Do you have what it takes? Let's find out as we march back to the training field.

GSF CADENCE

Attention! Forwaaaaaard, march! Let me hear your cadence, GSF.

God is great and God is good,
God is everywhere in your neighborhood.
Sound off, 1, 2
Sound off, 3, 4
Worship Him, give glory to His name,
From the beginning to the end, He's the same.
Sound off, 1, 2
Sound off, 3, 4
All hail to God the Commander in Chief,
In His Son is where we place our belief.
Sound off, 1, 2
Sound off, 3, 4
Send a signal, send a flare,
Lift your voice to the Lord in prayer!
Sound off, 1, 2
Sound off, 3, 4!

Way to march, soldiers! We are soooo proud of you! Now that we are back on the training field, let's pick up where we left off yesterday.

We discovered that prayer begins with worship of the Father. Do you know what worship is? To worship someone is to acknowledge his worth, to give him the honor and reverence that is due to him. It is praising God for WHO He is. This is what Jehoshaphat did before he ever asked God to help him. He began his prayer by reminding God of WHO He is.

Let's take a look at Daniel 4:34-35 printed out on the next page:

34 But at the end of that period, I, Nebuchadnezzar, raised my eyes toward heaven and my reason returned to me, and I blessed the Most High and praised and honored Him who lives forever; for His dominion is an everlasting dominion, and His kingdom endures from generation to generation. **35** All the inhabitants of the earth are accounted as nothing, but He does according to His will in the host of heaven and among the inhabitants of earth; and no one can ward off His hand or say to Him, "What have You done?"

WHERE does Nebuchadnezzar raise his eyes?

toward heaven

WHAT does he do to the Most High?

he blessed him.

WHAT does the Most High do?

"He does according to the earth in the host of heaven."

Did Nebuchadnezzar acknowledge God's worth? Yes

Yes, in this passage we see Nebuchadnezzar raising his eyes to heaven while he blesses and honors God, just like Jesus taught His disciples to do. Let's take another look at the first sentence in the Lord's Prayer: "Our Father who is in heaven, hallowed be Your name."

This sentence not only shows us God is our Father, but it is also a reminder that God lives in heaven and controls all the affairs of the universe. It shows us HOW God's name is to be treated. His name is to be hallowed. That means God's name is to be treated as holy. It is very special. It is to be reverenced above all others.

WHY? Because of WHO God is. He is our Commander in Chief, the absolute Ruler, the One with all power and might. Think about how a soldier responds to his commanding officer. A soldier snaps to attention and salutes his commanding officer with his right hand whenever he comes into the officer's presence to show his respect. Does he speak to his commanding officer any way he pleases? No way! A soldier responds to his commander by saying "Sir."

So just as a soldier salutes his commander in chief to show him the respect he deserves when he comes into his presence,

we need to approach our Commander in Chief with honor and respect. When we pray, we are to come into His presence by worshiping Him and praising His name.

Now look at what God tells Moses in Exodus 20:7, printed out below:

> *You shall not take the name of the LORD your God in vain, for the LORD will not leave him unpunished who takes His name in vain.*

WHAT does God tell Moses they are not to do?

<u>You shall not take the name of the Lord in vain</u>

WHAT will happen if they do?

<u>They will be punished</u>

WHY? Do you know? Taking God's name in vain is the opposite of hallowing it. When you take God's name in vain, you are disbelieving, denying, and distorting the truth about God. The name of the Lord is not just a title, but it is how God makes Himself known to us. His name tells us WHO He is. It tells us about His character.

When you don't believe what God says about Himself, then you are taking His name in vain because you are thinking wrong thoughts about Him. An example of disbelieving God would be to say, "God doesn't care about my needs." Did you know one of God's names means He is our Provider? So when you say, "God doesn't care about my needs," you are thinking wrong thoughts about God. You are disbelieving Him and taking His name in vain.

Another way to take His name in vain is by swearing or speaking His name in a casual, slang way. As Christians we have to be careful that we don't use God's name in a careless or bad way that does not treat Him as the holy God that He is. To violate God's name is to violate God.

HOW do you treat God's name?

- Do you hallow—respect and honor—His name?

Or
- Do you take His name in vain? Do you swear? Do you use His name in a casual way? Do you disbelieve WHO He says He is?

Tell HOW you treat God's name.

I treat his name in respect and don't sware at all

Now that we have discovered the importance of God's name, we need to find out some of His names. HOW can we honor and praise God if we don't know WHO He is?

Let's take a look at some of God's names and discover WHAT they mean so we can worship our Commander in Chief by praising His name. Grab those training manuals and look up the following scriptures to solve our crossword puzzle and find out how awesome our Commander in Chief is.

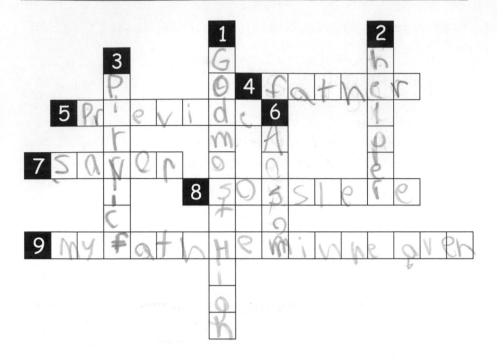

God's name is El Elyon. Look up and read Genesis 14:18-20.

WHAT is God called in these verses?

1. (Down) _God most High_

(Place all three of these words together in your crossword puzzle.)

This means that God is sovereign. He is the One in control. God is the Ruler of all. What He says, He will do. What He plans will come to pass. God is over the entire earth. We saw this name for God earlier when we looked at Nebuchadnezzar in Daniel 4:34-35.

God's name is Jehovah Rapha. Look up and read Exodus 15:26. WHAT is the Lord?

2. (Down) The Lord is your _helper_ .

God is our Physician. He can heal our bodies and our souls. He is the only One who can heal us from sin.

God's name is Elohim. Look up and read Genesis 1:1.

WHAT did God do in the beginning? He _____ the heavens and the earth. So WHAT does this show us about God?

3. (Down) God is _P_ _i_ _r_ _f_ _i_ _x_ _t_ (retacor) (Unscramble the word in the parentheses and place the letters in the blanks, then put this answer in your crossword puzzle.)

God's name is Jehovah Nissi. Look up and read Exodus 17:9-15.

Exodus 17:15 WHAT do we see about the Lord?

4. (Across) The Lord is my _father_.

A banner was a standard. In ancient times, sometimes a banner was a pole with an ornament that glittered in the sun. Today a banner is like a flag. The banner was carried out front ahead of the soldiers to indicate the line of march or the rallying point on the battlefield.

In Exodus 17:9-15 we see that when Israel fought against Amalek, Moses held God's staff up (His banner) and Israel prevailed. But when he grew tired and put down God's staff, they started losing.

After the fight was over and Israel had won, Moses built an altar and named it "the Lord is My Banner" to show that the battle was the Lord's. Victory came when the Lord was lifted up. This name of God shows us that God goes before us in battle just like the banner goes before the soldiers.

God is our victory on the battlefield. When we come against the enemy, we are not to surrender. We are to put on the armor of God, raise our banner, and fight. We are part of God's Special Forces. He is our banner; we are to be strong in the Lord and the strength of His might (Ephesians 6:10).

God's name is Jehovah Jireh. Look up and read Genesis 22:14. WHAT did Abraham call the name of the place?

5. (Across) The Lord will ___Prievide___.

God as Jehovah Jireh not only provided for our salvation by sending Jesus to die for our sins, but He also supplies all our needs. He comes to our aid when we are hurt or in trouble, strengthening us when we are weak, as well as giving us jobs, clothing, and food to eat. God is our Provider.

God's name is Jehovah Shammah. Look up and read Ezekiel 48:35. WHAT was the name of the city?

6. (Down) The Lord is _____.

God's name shows us that He is always there. When you are hurt and you think you have been forgotten and forsaken, then you need to remember that God's name, Jehovah Shammah, shows that you are not alone. You have not been forgotten. The almighty God of the universe is with you. He is there.

God's name is Jehovah Shalom. Look up and read Judges 6:24. WHAT is the Lord's name?

7. (Across) The Lord is _____.

The only place we can truly find peace is with our Lord God. When we are afraid and go through the hard and difficult times, we need to remember that God is our peace and run to Him.

God's name is Jehovah Raah. Look at Psalm 23:1.

WHAT is the Lord?

8. (Across) The Lord is my _____, I shall not want.

God shows us over and over in His Word that we are like sheep. Did you know that sheep are the most helpless, timid, defenseless animals and need constant care and attention? That's why we need a shepherd. We need God's loving hand to lead and guide us, to take care of all our needs and protect us from harm, just like the shepherd takes care of his sheep.

God's name is Jehovah Tsidkenu. Look up and read Jeremiah 23:6 WHAT is God's name in this verse?

9. (Across) The Lord is ___my___ ___father in heaven___.
(Put both of these words together in your crossword puzzle.)

God's name shows that He is our righteousness. To be righteous is to be right with God, to do what God says is right, to live according to His standards. HOW does God make us righteous? WHO died on a cross to save us from sin? Because of Jesus' sacrifice of dying on the cross and paying for our sin, we can be made right with God, Jehovah Tsidkenu.

Did you know that our Commander in Chief had all these names? Isn't it awesome to see how God's name reveals WHO He is? Practice all that you have learned in the field today by learning the nine descriptions of God below. We have also given you the Hebrew names inside the parentheses, but you don't have to learn them unless you want to.

God is Creator (Elohim), God Most High (El Elyon), God Our Righteousness (Jehovah Tsidkenu), Provider (Jehovah Jireh), Shepherd (Jehovah Raah), Peace (Jehovah Shalom), Our Banner (Jehovah Nissi), Healer (Jehovah Rapha), and God Is There (Jehovah Shammah).

Keep practicing by saying these names three times every day until you have them hidden in your heart, so that you will know your God and be able to worship Him in prayer.

Great drill practice! By the way, have you practiced Jesus'

code (the Lord's Prayer) and the titles that go with each subject? Don't forget to keep practicing those drills, too, as you
complete your training to become a soldier for God's Special
Forces. Outstanding!

DOWNRANGE TRAINING

"Attention!" commanded Captain Bryant. "Today we will
spend time working on exercises that will prepare you to be
sent downrange. Downrange is a dangerous overseas field
mission. God's A team needs to be fully equipped for any situation or circumstance, especially those hard and difficult
times that come with the territory of being a part of God's
Special Forces and serving our Commander in Chief.

"A GSF soldier needs to know how to handle a crisis.
WHOM would you turn to in a time of crisis: yourself, other
soldiers, or your Commander in Chief?"

Let's find out how a king named Hezekiah handles a crisis
that threatens his kingdom. Grab those rucksacks and prepare
to move out. But first you need to do WHAT? That's right,
soldier. Put a call in to the Commander in Chief and Papa-
Romeo-Alpha-Yankee. Do you know what that means? Papa-
Romeo-Alpha-Yankee are words that stand for different letters
of the alphabet. The Army uses these to spell words when
they communicate because it is very important that they
understand exactly what is being communicated, and some
letters of the alphabet sound the same, depending on your
accent and the quality of your radio communication.

Take a look at the Army Chart on the next page to discover
what Papa-Romeo-Alpha-Yankee stands for by writing the letter for each word in the blanks below.

P   R   A   Y
___   ___   ___   ___
Papa - Romeo - Alpha - Yankee

Now open up your line of communication. Then we will get started on the training exercises.

We're good to go. Our first assignment in learning how a GSF soldier handles a crisis is to take a look at Isaiah 36. But first we need to put ourselves in context.

At this time in history the nation of Israel has been divided into two kingdoms: the Northern Kingdom of Israel, which was made up of ten tribes; and the Southern Kingdom of Judah, which was made up of two tribes, Judah and Benjamin. Assyria has already captured the Northern Kingdom and is now threatening the Southern Kingdom.

Keep this in mind as you head to your Observation Worksheet on page 159. Read Isaiah 36 and mark the following key words. Don't forget to mark any pronouns that go with the key words, too! Also mark anything that tells you WHEN with a green clock like this: 🕐 and anything that tells you WHERE by double-underlining the WHERE in green.

Rabshakeh (color it orange)   King Hezekiah (color it light-green)

Sennacherib, king of Assyria (color it brown)

deliver (delivered) (draw a blue circle and color it red)

Now let's do some observation. Let's ask the 5 W's and an H.

Isaiah 36:1 WHEN did Sennacherib, the king of Assyria, come up against the cities of Judah to seize them?

In the ___fourteenth___ year of King ___Hezekiahs___

Isaiah 36:2 WHOM did the king of Assyria send to King Hezekiah with a large army?

___Assyria___

Isaiah 36:3 WHO came out to hear what Rabshakeh had to say?

___Eliakim___

Isaiah 36:4-14 Is Rabshakeh threatening to take the city?

___Yes___

Isaiah 36:14 WHAT does Rabshakeh tell them that Hezekiah will not be able to do?

___Hezkiah cant save you___

Isaiah 36:15 In WHOM does Hezekiah trust?

___Lord___

Isaiah 36:18-20 WHAT is Rabshakeh's attitude toward God?

___not believing___

Isaiah 36:21 HOW did they respond?

They remaind silent

WHY did they respond the way they did?

The king said not to answer Him

Isaiah 36:22 To WHOM did Eliakim, Shebna, and Joah run with the words of Rabshakeh?

Hezekiah

Rabshakeh came to Jerusalem with a large army to threaten King Hezekiah and his people. He told the people to not listen to Hezekiah when Hezekiah tells them that the Lord will deliver them because no one had been able to stop the king of Assyria. HOW did the people respond? Did they obey their king? _Yes_

Yes. The king said not to answer him, and they didn't. Then Eliakim, Shebna, and Joah ran to WHOM? Straight to their k  g, their commander in chief. Isn't that awesome! A very real crisis, and these guys headed straight to their king!

Now WHAT will be King Hezekiah's course of action? We'll find out when we rendezvous back here at 0600 hours to continue our downrange training.

DISCOVERING THE KING'S COURSE OF ACTION

Okay, soldiers, it's time to get started on another day in the field so that we will know what to do in times of crisis. We need to be fully trained and on alert so that our Commander in Chief can send us downrange on a special mission at a moment's notice.

Let's get started. Did you remember to Papa-Romeo-Alpha-Yankee? Then grab your gear as you take another look at King Hezekiah to uncover his COA (course of action) during a crisis that threatened his kingdom.

Turn to your Observation Worksheet on page 162 and move out. Read Isaiah 37 and mark the key words, along with any pronouns. Don't forget to mark anything that tells you WHEN with a green clock like this: 🕐 and anything that tells you WHERE by double-underlining the <u>WHERE</u> in green.

Rabshakeh (color it orange)   King Hezekiah (color it green)

Sennacherib, king of Assyria (color it brown)

Isaiah (color it blue)

deliver (delivered) (draw a blue circle and color it red)

prayer (draw a purple 👃 and color it pink)

remnant (draw a blue box with a line through it)

Now continue your observations to see the king's COA. Ask those 5 W's and an H.

Isaiah 37:1 WHAT does King Hezekiah do when he hears Rabshakeh's words?

He ___tore___ his ___close___.

He ___put___ himself with ___Sacclouth___ and

entered the ___Temple___ of the ___Lord___.

Isaiah 37:2 To WHOM does King Hezekiah send Eliakim and Shebna?

___Liholing Freest___

Isaiah 37:3-4 WHAT did they ask Isaiah to do?

offer a ___Sacriefie___ for the ___Lord___ that is left

Isaiah 37:6 WHAT did Isaiah tell them to tell King Hezekiah?

___The Lord says do not be afraid___

Isaiah 37:8-10 WHAT message does Rabshakeh send King Hezekiah?

"Do not let your ___faith___ in whom you trust ___in___

you, saying, '___/___ will not be given into the

hand of the ___Lord___ of ___Chist___.' Behold,

you have heard what the kings of Assyria have done to all

of the lands, __of__ them completely. So will you be __yours__?"

Isaiah 37:14 HOW did Hezekiah respond? WHAT did he do with the letter?

__Yes he did__

Isaiah 37:15 WHAT did Hezekiah do?

__he prayed__

Isaiah 37:16-20 HOW does Hezekiah approach God?

_____

HOW does Hezekiah's prayer parallel the Lord's Prayer? HOW are the two prayers alike?

__by pran__

Isaiah 37:16 WHAT name of God does Hezekiah use in his prayer?

__Lord all mitie__

This name for God is Jehovah-sabaoth, which means "the Lord of hosts." This name shows God as our Deliverer. When we have failed, when we are inadequate, when there is no other help, we have Jehovah-sabaoth, the Lord of hosts. We need to run to Him. He is our Deliverer.

Wow, just look at how King Hezekiah handled his crisis! He didn't say, "I am the king. I can handle this," nor did he panic and run away. Instead, he ran straight to the Lord of hosts with the letter he had received and spread it out before the Lord and worshiped Him.

He told God, "Look, Lord, I know that You alone are God over all the kingdoms of earth. But just listen to what Sennacherib, the king of Assyria, is saying. He says You can't deliver us, that he has devastated all the other nations, and we will be next."

Then after worshiping and telling God what has happened, Hezekiah specifically asks God to deliver them so that all the kingdoms of the earth would know that He alone is God.

WHAT were the results? Take a look at Isaiah 37:21-38. HOW did God answer King Hezekiah's prayer?

Isaiah 37:31 There is a surviving ___Lord___ of the house of Judah that will take ___The___ downward and ___make___ ___it___ upward.

Isaiah 37:33-34 The king of Assyria will not come to this ___place___ or shoot an ___arae___ there; and he will not come before it with a ___st i c___, or throw up a ___raved___ ramp against it.

Isaiah 37:35 God will ___enter___ the city to ___fix___ it.

Isaiah 37:36 The angel of the Lord struck

working in the camp of the Assyrians, and in the morning they were _safe_.

Isaiah 37:37-38 WHAT happened to Sennacherib, the king of Assyria?

_____

WHAT a powerful prayer! God saves the remnant that is left. He doesn't allow the king of Assyria to come and take the city. Instead, He defends and saves the city. He sends an angel to kill 185,000 of the Assyrians. Then when the king of Assyria leaves and goes home, his sons kill him.

HOW will you handle the next crisis when your Commander in Chief sends you "downrange"?

WHAT if one of your friends at school criticizes you or makes fun of you? WHAT will you do? Get mad? Hit him? Make fun of him? Or just ignore him? Write out WHAT you would do.

they get cut down with a sord

Now think about what we saw Eliakim, Shebna, and Joah do yesterday. They did not answer. They ran straight to their king.

WHAT did King Hezekiah do? He ran to God and worshiped Him. Isn't that amazing? Then he told God what the king of Assyria said and asked God to deliver them.

WHO is your king, your Commander in Chief? _God_

The next time you are in a difficult situation, such as someone making fun of you, run straight to God and worship Him: "I will give thanks to You, for I am fearfully and wonderfully made" (Psalm 139:14).

Don't let the kids who act like Rabshakeh and the king of Assyria get to you. Remember WHO God is. He is omniscient— that means He knows everything. He heard what those kids said. He is the Lord of hosts. He is your Deliverer. His name is Jehovah Shammah. He is there with you. And don't forget that He is your Creator. He made you special and loves you just the way you are!

Now as you take a break to eat those MREs, spend some time and Whiskey-Oscar-Romeo-Sierra-Hotel-India-Papa your Commander in Chief!

KEEPING A LOG

You did an awesome job out in the field yesterday developing your crisis communication skills! Let's replenish our water supply and grab our training manuals so we can continue our field exercises, learning how to worship our Commander in Chief and how to keep a log.

As we studied Hezekiah's prayer yesterday, did you notice that he did not worship God by repeating the same words over and over, such as saying, "Praise You, God, praise You God"? Instead, we see him praising God by rehearsing God's character and ways.

When the heathen worshiped their gods, they worked themselves into a frenzy, chanting the same words over and over. But that is not the way God wants to be worshiped. Remember what we learned in Matthew 6:7, where Jesus told His disciples not to use meaningless repetition. We are not to just repeat words or phrases to worship God.

Now there are verses in the Bible where repetition is used, but it is used to show the absolute truth of something, such as when the seraphim call out to God in Isaiah 6, "Holy, Holy, Holy, is the LORD of Hosts." This is not meaningless repetition;

instead, these words are repeated three times simply to state
the ultimate truth of the holiness of God.

Now let's hit the field and find out how Jeremiah and
Daniel, two of God's Special Forces soldiers, approached the
Commander in Chief.

Look up and read Jeremiah 32:16-25.

HOW does Jeremiah approach God?

By Praising Him.

Does Jeremiah describe God's qualities and remind God
of the things He has done as he worships, or does he
repeat the same praise words over and over?

Yes.

Look up and read Daniel 2:19-23. HOW did Daniel
respond to God when he received his answer in a night
vision?

Daniel 2:19 Daniel ___*Praised*___ the God of heaven.

Daniel 2:23 Daniel gives t *h a n k* s and p *r a i s* e
to God because God has given him w _ *sd* _ *o* m and
p *o w e* r and made known his request to understand
Nebuchadnezzar's dream.

So HOW did Daniel bless God—by vainly repeating the
same words, or by rehearsing the character traits of God
in his prayer?   *Identifying*

Look up and read Daniel 9:3-19. HOW did Daniel seek the Lord in this prayer?

Daniel 9:3 By _turning_ and _pleading_ with _Him_, _prayr_, and _patishion_.

Daniel 9:4 WHAT else did Daniel do in prayer? HOW did he open his prayer?

"Alas, O Lord, the _Great_ and _AOUSom_ God"

WHAT is this called? (Unscramble the word in the parentheses and place it in the blanks.) Daniel _praised_ (rapiesd) God.

Daniel 9:4-5 Then Daniel said, "We have s _i_ _n_ _n_ _e_ d, committed _rong_, acted _wickedly_ and _rebelled_."

WHAT is this? (Unscramble the word in the parentheses and place it in the blanks.) Daniel _confessed_ (oncefssde) their sins.

Daniel and Jeremiah both approached God by worshiping Him and praising Him for WHO He is and WHAT He had done, not by repeating vain words over and over. In the last prayer of Daniel's, we not only see Daniel worshiping God, but we also see that as Daniel worships he humbles himself before the Lord by fasting and putting on sackcloth and ashes. After he worships God, he confesses their sins. Daniel pleads with God for His forgiveness, asking God to hear his requests not because he deserved it, but because of WHO God is—God is a compassionate God.

If you were the one who was being worshiped, which would you prefer: praise and worship like Daniel and Jeremiah's that shows God's character, ways, and promises, or someone repeating, "Praise You, God" over and over? Remember, to worship someone is to acknowledge his or her worth. Which way honors God's worth?

_____

So if we are going to honor God for WHO He is, WHAT do we have to know? That's right—we have to know God, and God reveals Himself to us HOW? in His W__o_r__ d

Now that we have the know-how that we are to approach the Commander in Chief in worship by hallowing His name, by humbling ourselves and rehearsing His character, His ways, and promises, we need to practice our communication skills.

But first we need to learn how to keep a log. Did you know that every communication that comes into the command center is recorded in a log and kept in a logbook? It's very important for the command center to have a record of every communication sent out and received.

A GSF's logbook will not only keep a record of a soldier's communications with his Commander in Chief, but it will also be an encouragement in a time of crisis as he looks over the communications and is reminded just WHO his Commander in Chief is and HOW He has answered his prayers in the past to strengthen his faith.

So, soldiers, the first thing you will need is a blank logbook. You can use a three-ring binder (notebook) and add white pages to it, or you can buy a small notebook and decorate it with markers and stickers, or you can make one of your own. If you want to make your own, check out the supply list and instructions below.

Supply List

Two pieces of 8½ x 11 cardboard

At least 10-15 pieces of 8½ x 11 construction paper

10-15 pieces of 8½ x 11 white paper

Glue or glue stick, scissors, pencils, colored pencils,

Pen, markers, ribbon, a hole punch

Fabric or contact paper

- Take the two pieces of cardboard and cover them with fabric or contact paper. (If you don't have any cardboard, you can use two pieces of construction paper and decorate your cover using markers, pictures, or stickers.)

- Next, take your white paper and cut it so that it will fit on your construction paper, leaving a colored border.

- Glue your white paper to your construction paper.

- Punch three holes on the left side of your two pieces of cardboard and on your construction paper pages with your hole puncher.

- Put your logbook together by putting your construction paper pages in between your two decorated cardboard (or construction paper) covers.

- Cut three pieces of ribbon and insert a piece in each one of the three holes and tie it securely to hold your logbook together.

Now that you have either made or bought a logbook, let's get to work. Open your logbook and title your first page "Praise and Worship." Be as creative as you want. Use markers, colored pencils, pens, stickers, and pictures to title and decorate your page.

Next, start a list naming things you know about God so you can praise and worship Him. You can write down the names of God that you have learned like Elohim, God You are the Creator, You made heaven and earth. Then you could draw or glue a picture of something that God has created: the sun, animals, trees, people, etc.

You can read Psalms and write down what you learn about God. You can list some of the things you learned about God in Hezekiah's prayer, or you could go through the alphabet and think of praises for each letter of the alphabet. For the letter *A* (Alpha) you could write, "God, You are so awesome. God, You are almighty. God, You are amazing, etc. And then move on to the next letter of the alphabet.

Have fun and be artistic. Once you have finished recording your praises, put your know-how to work as you open up the lines of communication and worship God by praising the traits you have recorded in your logbook.

Great work, soldier! You are on your way to becoming a communications specialist!

OVERCOMING OBSTACLES

Hold on tight, soldier! You are doing great—just a little more. You almost have it. Pull hard. You can do it! All right! You made it to the top of the wall. Now take a deep breath and finish the obstacle course.

Whew! That was tough, but you did it! You

scaled the wall and completed the course. Pull out your CamelBak hydration system (your water bag). Take a drink of water and catch your breath before we get started on our next training assignment to uncover any obstacles that may hinder communication with the Commander in Chief.

Don't forget your daily communication check. Then jump into the

Jeep and pull out those maps and training manuals. Keep your eyes open as we look for obstacles while we navigate the lay of the land.

Now that we are on the move, think about what we have discovered so far as we have deciphered the first sentence in the special code of the Lord's Prayer. HOW do we approach the Commander in Chief? WHAT do we call Him as we open in prayer? Our F __ __ __ __ __.

WHOM do you call *Father, Daddy,* or *Dad?* Isn't it the man that you belong to in your family? You are your father's child either by birth or adoption. So HOW do we have the right to call the almighty, all-powerful God of the universe our Father? WHAT makes us His child?

Let's find out. Turn to your Observation Worksheet on page 165 to John 3. Read John 3:1-18 and answer the 5 W's and an H.

John 3:3 HOW do we see the kingdom of God?

_____

John 3:4 WHAT questions did Nicodemus ask?

"How can a man be _____ when he is _____?

He cannot enter a _____ time into his

mother's _____ and be _____, can he?"

John 3:5-6 WHAT is Jesus' answer?

"Unless one is _____ of _____ and the

_____ he cannot enter the kingdom of God. That

which is born of the _____ is _____,

and that which is born of the _____ is _____."

John 3:9-10 Does Nicodemus understand what it means to be born again? ____ Yes ____ No

Nicodemus came to Jesus at night because he had questions and knew that Jesus had come from God. When Jesus tells Nicodemus that he has to be born again to see God's kingdom, he is confused. Nicodemus doesn't understand how a man can go back inside his mother and be born again. Jesus tells him that He is not talking about being born of the flesh—the birth that happens when we are born as a baby. Instead, He is talking about a spiritual birth.

HOW does this spiritual birth happen? Let's find out.

Read John 3:16 HOW do you have eternal life?

_____

Now look at John 1:12-13 printed out below:

But as many as received Him, to them He gave the right to become children of God, even to those who believe in His name, who were born, not of blood nor of the will of the flesh nor of the will of man, but of God.

WHEN you receive Jesus and believe in His name,

WHAT right is given to you?

To become _____ of _____

HOW are we born of Him?

Born, not of _____, nor of the will of the _____

nor of the will of _____, but of _____

Does this sound like a spiritual birth, since it is not of the flesh? ____ Yes ____ No

Look at Ephesians 1:13-14 printed out below:

> *In Him, you also, after listening to the message of truth, the gospel of your salvation—having also believed, you were sealed in Him with the Holy Spirit of promise, who is given as a pledge of our inheritance, with a view to the redemption of God's own possession, to the praise of His glory.*

WHOM are we sealed with after we listen to the message of truth, believe, and are saved?

You were sealed in _____. WHO is this "Him"?

The _____ _____ of promise

WHAT is the Holy Spirit given as a pledge of?

_____

Look at Romans 8:14-15:

> *For all who are being led by the Spirit of God, these are sons of God. For you have not received a spirit of slavery leading to fear again, but you have received a spirit of adoption as sons by which we cry out, "Abba! Father!"*

HOW are we sons of God?

_____

WHAT do we receive?

A spirit of _____ as _____

WHAT do we cry out?

_____

You are doing a great job at navigating the land! Now let's pull it all together and look for any obstacles that could hinder us from communicating with the Commander in Chief.

We know we are to come to God as our Father, and that to be able to call someone *Father* you have to be his child either by birth or adoption. So HOW does God become our Father?

We have to be b __ __ n   a __ __ __ n.

HOW do we do this? WHOM do we have to believe in

and accept as our Savior? __ __ __ __ __

WHEN we accept Jesus according to John 1:12, we are

given the right to be WHAT? _____ of _____

Isn't that *amazing?* We are adopted by God and get to be kids of the almighty, all-powerful King of the universe. We can cry out to Him. We have the awesome privilege of coming to Him in prayer because He is our Father. We belong to Him and are part of His family.

Now that we have looked at all the facts, do you see the obstacle? HOW can you come to God in prayer if He isn't your Father? That's hard, isn't it? But our training manuals show us very clearly there is only one way to be the King's kid.

Let's look up and read 1 John 5:11-15 in our training manual.

1 John 5:14 If we believe in the name of the Son (Jesus), WHAT is our confidence we have before Him?

"If we _____ anything according to His _____,

He_____us."

1 John 5:15 WHAT will we have?

_____

The confidence we have that God will answer our prayers is if we believe in His Son and become His child. God is a loving and compassionate God, but there is only one prayer that He is obligated to answer for someone who isn't His child. Do you know what that prayer is? It's when you pray and admit that you are a sinner and ask to be saved by receiving Jesus Christ as your Savior.

God loves you. He wants to be your Father. He wants you to be able to come to Him, to know Him, and to have a relationship with Him.

Is the line of communication open between you and the Commander in Chief? Is God your Father? Do you have the right to come to Him in prayer? Have you accepted God's gift of salvation? ____ Yes ____ No

If you have, then you have navigated the land and are ready to continue training on God's "Q" course.

But if you haven't received God's gift of salvation and you want to become His child and be adopted into His loving family, all you have to do is come to God and ask. You need to admit that you are a sinner (Romans 3:23—"For all have sinned and fall short of the glory of God"). Tell God that you are sorry for your sins and want to be a follower of Jesus Christ.

You can pray a prayer like this:

> *Thank You, God, for loving me and sending Your Son, Jesus Christ, to die for my sins. I am sorry for the things I have done wrong. I am repenting, changing my mind about my sins. Sin is wrong. I don't want to do things my way anymore. I want to receive Jesus Christ as my Savior, and now I turn my entire life over to You. Amen.*

You are now a part of God's family! You are God's child, and Jesus and the Holy Spirit will come to live in you (John 14:23). You can now call the Commander in Chief your Father. Wow!

Now that you have become a part of God's family, you will want to share this great news by telling other people that you have believed in Jesus Christ and are now a child of God.

Way to go, soldier. You have navigated the land, overcome the obstacles, and are ready to continue on the "Q" course to be a communications specialist with the Commander in Chief!

> *Therefore if anyone is in Christ, he is a new creature; the old things passed away; behold, new things have come* (2 Corinthians 5:17).

PLEDGING OUR ALLEGIANCE

Well done, soldiers. What an accomplishment! You have mastered the first sentence of Operation Prayer. As we continue in Phase II on God's "Q" course, we are ready for our next assignment. But first, don't forget to do WHAT? That's right: Papa-Romeo-Alpha-Yankee to your Commander in Chief.

Now take a look at your next assignment. WHAT is the second sentence that Jesus taught His disciples in His pattern for prayer?

_____ _____ _____

WHAT did we title it? _____

WHAT was Jesus trying to teach His disciples as He told them to pray for God's kingdom to come? Let's find out. First, let's look at the Army oath of enlistment:

> I do solemnly swear (or affirm) that I will support and defend the Constitution of the United States against all enemies, foreign and domestic;

that I will bear true faith and allegiance to the same; and that I will obey the orders of the president of the United States and the orders of the officers appointed over me, according to regulations and the uniform code of military justice. So help me, God.

When a soldier in the Army takes this oath, he is promising that he is loyal to his country and will obey his commander in chief. It is a promise that he will put the nation's welfare above his own.

A soldier's goal, passion, and purpose is to serve the commander in chief, to lay down his life for the good of his commander and his country. Could this be what Jesus meant as He taught His disciples about praying for His kingdom?

Let's uncover what it means to pledge our allegiance to our Father, the Commander in Chief. Sharpen your observation skills by studying the following passages and answering the 5 W's and an H.

Pull out your training manual and look up and read Philippians 3:20.

If you are a Christian, WHERE is your citzenship?

In _____

WHAT are we waiting for? A _____, the

Lord _____
(Circle these two words together as you do the word search on page 72.)

Turn back to your Observation Worksheet on Matthew 6 on page 153. Look at verse 33. WHAT are we to seek first?

His _____ and His _____

Now look at Mark 8:34 printed out below:

> *And He summoned the crowd with His disciples, and said to them, "If anyone wishes to come after Me, he must deny himself, and take up his cross and follow Me."*

WHAT did Jesus say you have to do to come after Him?

_____ yourself.

Take up your _____.

_____ Me.

Read Matthew 10:34-39.

> **34** Do not think that I came to bring peace on the earth; I did not come to bring peace, but a sword. **35** For I came to set a man against his father, and a daughter against her mother, and a daughter-in-law against her mother-in-law; **36** and a man's enemies will be the members of his household. **37** He who loves father or mother more than Me is not worthy of Me; and he who loves son or daughter more than Me is not worthy of Me. **38** And he who does not take his cross and follow after Me is not worthy of Me. **39** He who has found his life will lose it, and he who has lost his life for My sake will find it.

WHAT does Jesus expect? WHOM are you to love more: your family or Jesus?

_____

Matthew 10:39 WHAT do you need to lose for His sake?

Your _____

Does this mean Jesus doesn't want us to love our families? No! God makes it very clear in His Word that we are to love one another, and we are to honor and obey our mother and father. Jesus is saying that our allegiance is to Him first. We are to love Him above all other people including our earthly families and ourselves.

Read Luke 9:57-62:

> **57** As they were going along the road, someone said to Him, "I will follow You wherever You go." **58** And Jesus said to him, "The foxes have holes and the birds of the air have nests, but the Son of Man has nowhere to lay His head." **59** And He said to another, "Follow Me." But he said, "Lord, permit me first to go and bury my father." **60** But He said to him, "Allow the dead to bury their own dead; but as for you, go and proclaim everywhere the kingdom of God." **61** Another also said, "I will follow You, Lord; but first permit me to say good-bye to those at home." **62** But Jesus said to him, "No one, after putting his hand to the plow and looking back, is fit for the kingdom of God."

Jesus says to follow Him, but WHAT is their response? Look at verses 59 and 61. "first _____ me"

WHAT were they putting first: Jesus and His kingdom or their own desires? Their own _____

Let's look at one more verse—Colossians 1:18:

> *He is also head of the body, the church; and He is the beginning, the firstborn from the dead, so that He Himself will come to have first place in every-thing.*

The *He* in this passage is referring to Jesus. WHAT is Jesus' place to be in everything?_____

Now find the answers that you wrote in each blank starting on page 69 and circle them in the word search below.

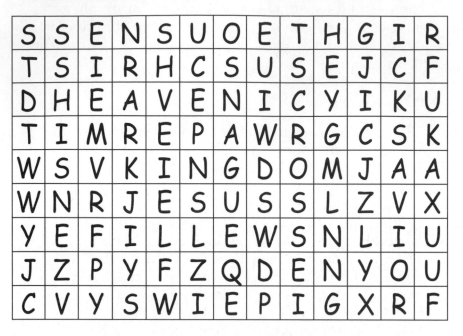

S	S	E	N	S	U	O	E	T	H	G	I	R
T	S	I	R	H	C	S	U	S	E	J	C	F
D	H	E	A	V	E	N	I	C	Y	I	K	U
T	I	M	R	E	P	A	W	R	G	C	S	K
W	S	V	K	I	N	G	D	O	M	J	A	A
W	N	R	J	E	S	U	S	S	L	Z	V	X
Y	E	F	I	L	L	E	W	S	N	L	I	U
J	Z	P	Y	F	Z	Q	D	E	N	Y	O	U
C	V	Y	S	W	I	E	P	I	G	X	R	F

Great observations, soldiers. Now WHAT about you?

• Are you putting God's kingdom first? _____

• Do you have time to play sports, watch TV, play computer games, e-mail, and talk on the phone, but no time to read God's Word or pray? Write out what you do.

_____

_____

• Do any of the things you like or do keep you from giving God first place? ____ Yes ____ No If the answer is yes, write out those things that you put before God.

_____

_____

- Are you willing to give up those things, follow Jesus, and give Him your all, the same way a soldier is willing to lay down his life for his country?

  _____

- So WHO is first, soldier: you and your desires, or God and His kingdom?

  _____

Now that you know what it means to pray for God's kingdom, pull out your logbooks and title your next page "Thy Kingdom Come, Allegiance to God's Kingdom." Then decorate this page like you did before using markers, colored pencils, pens, or stickers. Draw a picture of a throne with a crown over it and a GSF soldier pledging his allegiance.

If you are willing to follow Jesus and give Him your all, write out a prayer to your Father and promise Him your allegiance. Just keep it simple and share your heart. Tell Him that He is the sovereign Ruler over the universe and that you want to give Him and His kingdom first place in your life. Tell Him you are sorry for the times you put your desires before His.

Ask God to show you the areas in your life where you don't put Him first. Tell Him you want to deny yourself, to be courageous, to persevere in adversity. Tell Him you want to honor Him, to read His Word, and to talk to Him each day. Let Him know that you want to win the battle, you want His kingdom to come and for Jesus to rule and reign here on earth.

Way to march, soldier. Let's win the battle for God's kingdom!

FOLLOWING ORDERS

Head to the communication center, soldier. Captain Bryant is about to begin his briefing for our next mission.

"As we prepare to wrap up Phase II of 'Q' course training," Captain Bryant stated while he passed out our next assignments, "you need to work on ambushes, reconnaissance missions, and other tasks so that we have a clear evaluation of how you respond to orders and interact with team members before you are put under pressure on the battlefield. Pack those rucksacks, run an equipment check, and be ready to move out at 0900 hours."

Are you ready, soldier? Have you followed the captain's orders? Let's run an equipment check and check in with our Commander in Chief so we are prepared for our next mission out in the field.

WHAT is the third sentence of the Lord's Prayer?

_____ _____ _____ _____, _____ _____

_____ _____ _____ _____ _____.

WHAT title did you give it?_____

Do you know WHAT submission is? Look up the words *submission* and *submit* in a dictionary and then write out the meaning.

_____

_____

This third sentence in Jesus' special code on prayer— "Your will be done, on earth as it is in heaven"—teaches us that as we communicate with the Commander in Chief, we need to bow our knees and surrender to His will. It is saying to God, "I want Your will for my life instead of my will." A soldier's priority is to follow his commander's orders.

So how does a GSF soldier learn what he needs to know so he can obey his Commander in Chief? By studying his training manual—God's Word. Our training manual not only teaches us about our Commander in Chief, but it also communicates His will so that we can follow His orders and know exactly how He wants us to live.

You're good to go, so move 'em out, soldier. Grab your training manual and let's start discovering the Commander in Chief's will.

Look up and read John 6:40.

WHAT is the Father's will?

_____

Look up and read John 8:24.

WHAT happens if you do not do the Father's will and believe in Jesus?

_____

Look up and read 2 Peter 3:9.

Does God want anyone to perish? _____

Look up and read Acts 4:12.

Can we be saved any other way besides believing in

Jesus' name? _____

So can you come to God any way you want to or do you have to do it His way?

_____

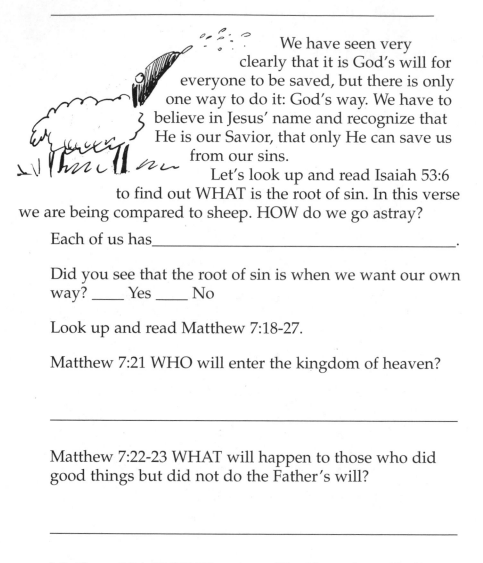

We have seen very clearly that it is God's will for everyone to be saved, but there is only one way to do it: God's way. We have to believe in Jesus' name and recognize that He is our Savior, that only He can save us from our sins.

Let's look up and read Isaiah 53:6 to find out WHAT is the root of sin. In this verse we are being compared to sheep. HOW do we go astray?

Each of us has_____.

Did you see that the root of sin is when we want our own way? ____ Yes ____ No

Look up and read Matthew 7:18-27.

Matthew 7:21 WHO will enter the kingdom of heaven?

_____

Matthew 7:22-23 WHAT will happen to those who did good things but did not do the Father's will?

_____

Matthew 7:24-25 WHO are you like if you hear God's words and act on them?

_____

Matthew 7:26-27 WHO are you like if you hear God's words but don't act on them?

_____

Look up and read 1 John 5:3-5.

1 John 5:3 WHAT does God want us to do?

_____

1 John 5:4 WHAT is the victory that overcomes the world?

_____

1 John 5:5 WHO overcomes the world?

He who believes that _____

Look up and read John 9:31.

WHOM does God hear?

_____

To be God's child and a part of His family, we have to be willing to do things God's way. Did you see that God wants everyone to be in His kingdom but that the only way to enter His kingdom is to do His will?

- Have you done the will of the Father? Have you accepted Jesus Christ as your Savior? ____ Yes ____ No

- WHO are you like? Are you like the wise man who hears Jesus' words and acts on them or the foolish man who hears Jesus' words but doesn't act on them?

_____

- Do you love the Father? Do you keep His command-ments?

_____

As we continue our mission, we need to remember what we saw in John 9:31—that God hears our prayers when we fear Him (which means to hallow or honor His name by reverencing Him) and by doing His will.

We want to keep the lines of communication open so that the Commander in Chief can receive our transmission. So pull out your logbook and title the next page "Your will be done, on earth as it is in heaven." You might want to glue a picture of yourself and write under it "Father, I surrender to Your will," or you could draw a picture of yourself bowing before your Commander in Chief in surrender.

Then write out a short prayer, praising and worshiping your Commander. Tell Him that you want to be like the wise man who built his house on the rock, you want to hear His words and act on them, you want Him to have control over your life so that your life will be built on knowing Him and seeking His will. Tell Him you want to be a member of His A team, to learn how to know and pray for His will.

All right! Now head back to the tent and catch some zzzzzz's. Tomorrow we continue our training to seek the will of our Commander in Chief.

3

SEEKING THE COMMANDER'S WILL

Good morning, soldiers! You are doing an awesome job learning how to use Jesus' special code so that you can be a communications specialist with the Commander in Chief. This week we will continue in the field as we survey the land and keep a lookout for any ambushes.

So put on your camouflage gear and lace up those boots. We are ready to survey the territory.

WATCHING FOR AMBUSHES

"Prayer Warrior 1, this is Chief. Sit rep. Over."

"Chief, this is Prayer Warrior 1. Routine. All quiet. Over."

"Roger, Prayer Warrior 1. Continue. Over."

"Wilco. Out."

Now that we have received confirmation from our Commander in Chief we need to proceed with Operation Prayer. As we scout the area, let's review the procedures from the first three topics in our communications expert's special code, the Lord's Prayer.

1. Prayer is a privilege for those who have faith and believe God. They have accepted Jesus Christ as their Savior and have been born again in God's family and have the right to come to their Father in prayer. HOW do we approach our Father? By honoring and worshiping Him for WHO He is, His character, His ways and WHAT He has done for us—by praising His name.

2. Prayer requires giving our allegiance to God and His kingdom. We give Him first place in our life and in all that we do.

3. Prayer requires submission. We tell God that all we want is His will. We ask Him to help us surrender control of our lives, study His Word, observe His commandments, to seek and do His will.

Now let's take a look at some promises in the Bible on prayer.

Look up and read John 14:14.

WHAT is the promise that Jesus makes in this verse?

_____

Look up and read John 16:24. WHAT is the promise?

_____

Look up and read Matthew 17:20.

WHAT happens if you have faith?

_____

_____

Look up and read Mark 11:24. WHAT happens when you pray, ask, and believe?

_____

_____

WHAT do all of the verses promise us, soldier? If we have faith, ask, and believe we will get our requests. Is that true? Yes, we know that these promises are true because they are found in God's Word. Second Timothy 3:16 tells us that all Scripture is inspired by God. That means it is "God-breathed." Scripture comes directly from God and does not contain any errors.

Wow—so we can just name what we want in faith, claim it in prayer, and we'll have it, right? Be careful, soldier. Watch out for that trap! You are about to be ambushed! Sometimes Christians pray, asking in faith, and God doesn't answer that prayer. They are devastated and confused because they don't understand why their prayer wasn't answered.

WHY aren't those prayers answered if this person is a Christian and God's Word tells us we can ask and we will receive? It's really very easy, soldier. WHAT did we learn in the third sentence in Jesus' special code on prayer? HOW are we to pray? Write this third sentence once again from Jesus' code on prayer.

_____

Now think about this: WHAT if what you have asked for in faith isn't God's will? Will God answer those prayers?

_____ Yes _____ No

Take a look at 1 John 5:14-15 again. It's printed out below:

This is the confidence which we have before Him, that, if we ask anything according to His will, He hears us. And if we know that He hears us in whatever we ask, we know that we have the requests which we have asked from Him.

HOW are we to ask so that God hears us? Find out by decoding our puzzle below. Color the spaces red that have a dot in them.

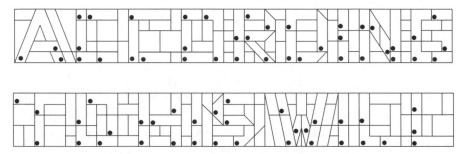

Now write out the answer to the puzzle. HOW we are to ask so that God hears us?

_____

So, soldier, if we ask this way, will we receive our

requests? _____

Absolutely! What God promises us in His Word is true. God is a faithful God. He always keeps His promises. But what we ask for has to be lined up with His will. God will hear us and answer our prayers, but only when our prayers line up with His character and His ways.

Sometimes Christians pray for things that aren't God's will, so out of His love for us and to fulfill His purpose, His answer is no. It's not because we didn't have enough faith. It's simply because it wasn't His will. God is love and always acts in love. He will always do what is the best for us.

Now that we have avoided an ambush, let's get some prayer practice in with our Commander in Chief, submitting to His will:

Father, thank You for giving us this special prayer code from Jesus so that we can know how You want us to pray.

God, You are El Elyon, Most High God, and nothing is impossible for You! I am Your child and know that You hear me and will answer all my prayers. I know that sometimes I may ask for something that isn't Your will and that Your answer will be no in those circumstances. I trust You because You see the big picture that I can't always see. I know that You will answer my prayers as they fit into Your holy will.

Please help me to know Your will so I will know how to pray. Help me to remember that You are always faithful to your promises. When I ask in faith, I will receive if it is according to Your will. I give my life over to You and trust You, knowing that You love me and Your will is always the best! In Your Son Jesus' precious name. Amen.

AVOIDING THE TRAPS

Okay, soldiers, keep your guard up as we continue to scout the area for those hidden ambushes. It's very important for GSF soldiers to study their training manuals and follow their maps so they don't get caught in the enemy's trap. Have you checked in with the Commander in Chief? Good. Then lay low and pull out your training manuals as we continue on our mission.

Let's read Matthew 21:18-22 printed out below. Mark the following key words:

faith (purple book colored green)   doubt (color it black)

believe (believing) (color it blue)   say (color it orange)

> **18** Now in the morning, when He was returning to the city, He became hungry. **19** Seeing a lone fig tree by the road, He came to it and found nothing on it except leaves only; and He said to it, "No longer shall there ever be any fruit from you." And at once the fig tree withered. **20** Seeing this, the disciples were amazed and asked, "How did the fig tree wither all at once?" **21** And Jesus answered and said to them, "Truly I say to you, if you have faith and do not doubt, you will not only do what was done to the fig tree, but even if you say to this mountain, 'Be taken up and cast into the sea,' it will happen. **22** And all things you ask in prayer, believing, you will receive."

Now read Mark 11:23-24 and mark the same key words you marked before in Matthew.

> *Truly I say to you, whoever says to this mountain, "Be taken up and cast into the sea," and does not doubt in his heart, but believes that what he says is going to happen, it will be granted him. Therefore I say to you, all things for which you pray and ask, believe that you have received them, and they will be granted you.*

WHAT do we see from these passages of Scripture?

WHAT do we have to have? f __ __ __ __

WHAT are we not to do? d __ __ __ __

HOW are we to ask? b __ __ __ __ __ __ __ g

So if we took just these passages of Scripture in Matthew and Mark, could we convince people that all they had to do is have faith, don't doubt, and ask believing, and they would get what they prayed for? Yes. But is looking only at what these passages show us about prayer an ambush? Yes! WHY? Because these passages are just a small portion of God's Word. We can't pull out a passage of Scripture and use it any way we want to. God gave us the whole Bible, and we have to interpret (understand what it means) it by looking at how the whole Bible fits together.

That's what it means to look at context; you look at the setting where the verses are found. You look at the verses that come before the passage you are studying and the verses that come after the passage. Then you look at how it fits into the book you are studying, and how that fits into the whole Bible.

There is a very important rule that you need to know when you study the Bible for yourself, and that rule is: Scripture never contradicts Scripture! In fact, looking at other passages of Scripture and what they teach about prayer will help us understand more about the passage we are studying.

So if you want to understand prayer and how God hears and answers prayer, then you have to look at the whole Bible, and not at just one or two passages that have been taken out of context to suit someone's purpose. Remember what we saw yesterday? If we want God to answer our prayers, we have to ask HOW?

According to His (God's) _____

This is the key to having our prayers answered: asking according to God's will. Don't get ambushed and caught in a "name it and claim it" trap! For instance, some people teach that if you are a Christian, you can ask for anything you want in faith and you will get it.

Let's say you have an old, beat-up bike, and the chain is always coming off. Which prayer would be best? "God, I'm Your kid, and I know You don't want me riding this yucky old bike. So I am asking in faith for a brand-new mountain bike." Or, "God, You know everything. You know my bike is old and yucky. Every time I ride it, my chain comes off. I would like to have a new mountain bike. Maybe I could earn the money to buy a new one, or maybe I should have my old one fixed. Please show me what to do."

Do you see the difference in these two prayers? The first one is saying, "Because I'm Your kid and ask in faith, You will give me what I ask for." That's the "name it and claim it" trap. The second one says, "I am asking for what I want in faith, but I want what You think is best."

Jesus' teachings in Matthew and Mark are true. We are to ask in faith, but that faith comes by believing God and submitting to His will. Then God will hear us and give us our requests.

So HOW can you know if what you are praying for is God's will? We'll find out as we continue Operation Prayer.

RECON MISSION—DISCOVERING THE COMMANDER IN CHIEF'S WILL

Great work, soldiers! So far you have avoided the ambushes and traps that some soldiers fall into. Today we will work on a recon—a reconnaissance mission—inspecting the terrain so we can determine where to send our soldiers. Are you ready to head out? Then check your gear and grab your SATCOM to get the go-ahead from the Commander in Chief.

All right soldiers — move out!

Let's take another look at 1 John 5:14-15.

This is the confidence which we have before Him, that, if we ask anything according to His will, He hears us. And if we know that He hears us in what-ever we ask, we know that we have the requests which we have asked from Him.

WHAT is the condition to have God hear and answer our prayers?

_____

WHAT do we have before Him that shows we know God will answer our prayer when we meet His conditions? Unscramble the answer in the parentheses and place it in the blanks. (oncifdnece)

__ __ __ __ __ __ __ __ __ __

Isn't that awesome? We can be confident that God will answer our prayer when we ask according to His will. So HOW can we know His will? Let's find out by looking at another passage of Scripture.

Read John 15:7 printed out below:

If you abide in Me, and My words abide in you, ask whatever you wish, and it will be done for you.

WHAT are the conditions in this verse to asking and receiving?

If you _____ in Me and My words

_____ in you

The conditions in this verse are the answer to knowing God's will. In order to know God's will, you have to abide in Jesus and have His words abide in you.

WHAT does that word *abide* mean? To abide is "to be at home with, to dwell with." It means "to remain with or continue in, to endure." When you abide with someone, you get to know him. Think about the people who live in your house. Do you know their favorite food, what they like to do, and what they think is funny? HOW do you know these things? It's because you live with them and have gotten to know them, because they are a part of your family.

So HOW do we abide in Jesus and have His words abide in us? Jesus makes His home with and dwells in us when we believe in Him and accept Him as our Savior and become a part of God's family. We also receive a Helper, the Holy Spirit (John 14:26). The way we abide with Jesus and God is by getting to know them through spending time in Bible study and prayer. HOW do His words abide in us? By knowing what the Bible says. Remember, we saw that the Bible is "God-breathed." We can know God's words when we study and know what the Bible says.

> HOW much time do you spend praying and studying God's Word?

> _____

> Do you memorize His words and hide them in your heart?

> ____ Yes ____ No

To be part of God's A team, you need to spend time getting to know God each and every day. You're doing that right now by studying His Word and learning how to pray. The more you learn about God, His character, and His ways, the better you will know and understand what God's will is when you come to Him in prayer.

Your recon mission was successful! Now take a moment and check in with the Commander in Chief to ask Him to help you to always abide in Him. Ask Him to help you put Him first by praying, studying His Word, and seeking His will in all that you do every day!

GETTiNG iNTO POSiTiON

Good morning, soldiers. It's time to break camp and head out on another reconnaissance mission. As we study the terrain, we need to check in with our Commander in Chief to get our orders so that we will know the best way to position our soldiers. The success of this mission depends not only on how we position our soldiers, but also on where we position them. So are you good to go? Then let's review our plans and move out.

Have you noticed that so far in Operation Prayer our focus has been totally on God? First we discovered WHO He is— that He is our Father, a sovereign God who lives in heaven and rules over all the earth, that He is holy and His name is to be hallowed. We saw that we are to come into His presence by worshiping and honoring Him for WHO He is and WHAT He has done.

Once we have put our focus on God by worshiping Him, then we are ready to give Him our commitment to put Him first in our lives. Our next course of action is to surrender to our Commander-in Chief's will, to allow Him to have absolute control over our lives. This is just like a soldier who joins the armed forces, takes an oath, and lays aside any personal plans he might have in order to serve his country and his commander in chief.

Is it always easy as a member of God's Special Forces to put away our desires and serve our Commander in Chief? No! Even though we have been born again and are new creatures in Christ, we still live in fleshly bodies that are selfish and want their own way. Sometimes we will experience a struggle as we serve our Commander in Chief because we think we know what is best and want our way.

But is that true? WHO knows everything: you or God? Is God good? Does He love us and want what is best for us? So in WHOM do you want to place your trust: a rookie soldier who is still growing and learning, or an all-knowing, all-powerful Commander in Chief?

Let's gather some strategic information on how to position ourselves in times of struggle by taking a look at our communications expert as He prays to the Father in the Garden of Gethsemane.

Read Luke 22:41-44 printed out below. Double-underline in red everything that shows you what Jesus went through and what He was feeling.

41 And He withdrew from them about a stone's throw, and He knelt down and began to pray, **42** saying, "Father, if You are willing, remove this cup from Me; yet not My will, but Yours be done." **43** Now an angel from heaven appeared to Him, strengthening Him. **44** And being in agony He was praying very fervently; and His sweat became like drops of blood, falling down upon the ground.

Luke 22:44 WHAT emotion was Jesus feeling?

_____

WHAT happened to Jesus physically while He was praying very fervently?

_____

Luke 22:42 WHAT did Jesus ask God to do in this prayer?

_____

HOW did He ask the Father?

"Father, if You are _____."

After Jesus makes His request, does He submit to the Father's will? _____ Yes _____ No

WHAT are His words?

"Not _____ _____, but _____ be done."

Think about HOW Jesus was feeling and about what happened to Him physically. Was it easy for Jesus to surrender to the Father's will, or was it a struggle?

_____

   It was quite a struggle. Jesus even sweat drops of blood! Have you ever seen anyone sweat drops of blood? Our bodies are created in such a way that when we are under great stress, we will usually faint.

When we faint, it releases our body from stress and our blood pressure comes down. But if this doesn't happen, the blood pressure can go so high that the little capillaries in our head actually burst under the pressure, seeping blood, which mingles with the sweat. This causes a very horrible, horrible headache! Can you imagine this happening to you? Yet Jesus was under such tremendous physical stress that He actually sweat drops of blood, and God sent an angel to give Him strength.

WHY was Jesus in such agony? Look back at what He prayed for. He asked God to remove this cup. The cup was Jesus dying on a cross for the sins of the world. God would take all our sins, every single one that anyone ever committed or would commit, and place those sins on Jesus. Jesus would be made a curse to pay for the sins of you and me.

Then God would turn His back on Jesus because God is holy and cannot look upon sin. This would be the first time Jesus had ever been separated from His Father both physically and spiritually.

Did Jesus want to go through this hell? No! So He pleaded with His Father, asking God to remove the cup. But notice HOW He asks: "If You are willing, remove this cup from Me; yet not My will, but Yours be done." Even though Jesus doesn't want to go to the cross, He is willing to surrender His way to God's way. He is willing to do God's will, to obey His Father no matter what the cost. Isn't that awesome? Jesus not only worshiped His Father, but He also laid aside His rights as God to submit to His Father's will.

Do you want your way if it goes against what God thinks is best, His purpose and will for you?

WHAT would have happened if Jesus had not prayed for God's will? If He had decided the way was just too hard and that He didn't want to drink the cup God had given Him, WHERE would we be? We would be totally lost and dead in our sins, without any hope. Aren't you happy that Jesus did all things to please His Father and submitted to His will? It isn't always easy to give up our way for God's, but no matter how hard it is, we need to remember that God's way is always best!

Great work! Our soldiers are in just the right position. Tomorrow we will carry on as we continue to discover the Commander in Chief's will.

Before you hit the sack, pull out your logbooks and get some prayer practice in by writing a short prayer to the Commander in Chief on your page titled "Your will be done, on earth as it is in heaven." Ask God to give you the wisdom to know His will and the willingness to surrender in times of struggle, just like Jesus did.

EXECUTING THE COMMANDER IN CHIEF'S PLAN

"Prayer Warrior 1, this is Chief. Over."
"Chief, this is Prayer Warrior 1. Over."
"Prayer Warrior 1, ready to roll? Over."
"Chief, ready to roll. Over."
"Prayer Warrior 1. Execute. Out."
"Wilco. Out."

Move out, soldiers. Let's execute the Commander in Chief's plan.

HOW did we discover that a GSF soldier could know the Commander in Chief's plan? By communication, abiding in Him (getting to know God through prayer and His Word), and having His words abide in us.

But WHAT happens if our line of communication is full of static and we aren't sure of the Commander in Chief's plan? Are we stranded, or does He have a backup plan?

> Look up and read Romans 8:14. HOW are we led as sons of God?

_____

Now look up and read Romans 8:26-27.

Romans 8:26 WHO helps us in our weakness and intercedes for us when we don't know how to pray?

_____

Romans 8:27 HOW does the Spirit intercede for the saints (those who believe in Jesus)?

According to the _____

     Do you know what it means to intercede for someone? That means to plead on their behalf. These verses show us that when we don't know how to pray, the Holy Spirit (that God has given us as our Helper when we become His child) prays for us because He understands the will of God. Jesus told the disciples in John 14 that He would send a Helper, the Spirit of truth, to be with them so that they would not be left as orphans when He went back to heaven.
     God always has a plan. He has given us His Spirit, who knows His will and who will go to God on our behalf when we pray, seeking to know His will.
     Now that we know that God has provided a Helper to help lead us in His will, is there any way we can know the Commander in Chief's specific will?
     Let's take a look at Romans 12:1-2 printed out below:

> **1** Therefore I urge you, brethren, by the mercies of God, to present your bodies a living and holy sacrifice, acceptable to God, which is your spiritual service of worship. **2** And do not be conformed to this world, but be transformed by the renewing of your mind, so that you may prove what the will of God is, that which is good and acceptable and perfect.

Romans 12:1 HOW are we to present our bodies?

_____

_____

Romans 12:2 WHAT are we not to be?

_____

WHAT are we to be?

_____

WHY are we to do this?

So that you may prove _____

God shows us right in His Word in Romans 12:1-2 HOW we can know His specific will.

1. We have to present our bodies as a living sacrifice.

   WHAT does that mean? It means God wants us to lay our lives on the altar like the biblical sacrifices were laid on the altar. We are to lay down our lives sacrificially by giving God our lives and telling Him, "God, You can do with me as You please." We are to be like Jesus and say, "Not My will, Lord, but Yours be done."

2. We are not to be conformed to this world but transformed by the renewing of our minds. That means we are not to be squeezed into the world's mold, to be shaped by the way the world thinks. As we study God's Word we will be transformed, we will be changed. We

will lay aside what the world has told us is right, to line ourselves up with what God's Word says is right. Our minds will be made new so that we have the mind of Christ.

Now that you have discovered God's specific will:

- Are you willing to lay your life on the altar and let God have His way? ____ Yes ____ No

- Is your mind shaped by the world, or transformed by God's Word?

  _____

Kids will want you to talk like them, listen to the music they listen to, and wear the same kind of clothes they wear. They will not want you to dress or talk differently. They will want to squeeze you into their mold. But because you are a child of God, you are to be like God, and not like the world.

- WHAT kind of music do you listen to?

  _____

- HOW do you talk? WHAT kind of language do you use, especially when you are frustrated or angry?

  _____

• Does what you wear honor God, or do you wear what is considered to be "cool" so you can fit in with the crowd? Write out WHAT you do.

_____

• HOW do you treat other kids? Are you friends only with the "cool" and popular kids?

_____

Now take the time to communicate with the Commander in Chief. Pray and tell God that you don't want to be shaped by the world. Ask Him to show you the areas in your life where you have been shaped by the world and to help you turn away and be changed. Ask Him to renew your mind by knowing His truth. Ask God to show you how He wants you to live each day.

Outstanding recon! You have executed the Commander in Chief's plan.

SENDING AND RECEIVING COMMUNICATION FROM THE COMMANDER

"Listen up, soldiers," commanded Captain Bryant as he approached our campsite. "Captain Phillips will guide you on our mission today as you set up and use different types of radio equipment."

"Knowing and understanding how all of your communications gear works is critical as a communications specialist," stated Captain Phillips as he began his briefing. "When you are sent downrange on a difficult mission, you need to know how to communicate in that area regardless of the conditions. As we know, not all areas have a satellite transponder overhead, which means that you will not always be able to use your SATCOM radio.

"In these types of situations, where our high tech-equipment fails you will need to know how to use the "Turkey-43" radio sets. To use these sets, you have to be able to cut and string special wire antennas so that signals can bounce off the upper atmosphere, allowing you to fire off secure radio shots to anywhere in the world. So let's get busy, soldiers. Pack up your equipment. We'll head out at 0800 hours."

Are you packed and ready to go? Let's get started. We need to learn how to cut and string our antennas so that we can keep in touch with our Commander in Chief and discern His will.

So far in our training, we have seen that the two ways we can know God's will are to lay ourselves on the altar as a sacrifice and to know God's Word because God never acts contrary to His Word or His character.

Today as we hit the field to learn how to use our "Turkey-43's," we need to look at the third way we can know God's will. Let's take another look at John 15:7:

> *If you abide in Me, and My words abide in you, ask whatever you wish, and it will be done for you.*

WHAT needs to abide in you so that you can ask whatever you wish? My __ __ __ __ __

WHAT does it mean "My words abide in you"? Let's find out. We need to look at what *words* means in the Greek language, which was the original language that the New Testament (where John 15:7 is found) was written in. The

Greek word for *words* in John 15:7 is *rhema* (pronounced hray'-mah). This means "what is spoken, what is uttered in speech or writing."

In this reference in John 15:7, where it says, "and My words," it is saying that when we have a specific word, a scripture from God that shows us His will, we can ask whatever we wish, and it will be done for us.

So HOW does God give us this *rhema*, this specific scripture? As you spend time alone with God in prayer, worshiping Him, and presenting your body as a living sacrifice, you can cry out and ask God to show you His will. Then you have to quietly wait for God's Holy Spirit to lead you.

There are many ways that God speaks quietly to our hearts as He answers our cry of knowing His will in a specific situation. God could answer you as you have your quiet time, or He could direct you to a specific passage of Scripture as you read His Word, or He can simply remind you of a passage of Scripture that you have already hidden in your heart.

But you have to be careful! A *rhema*, a specific word from God, grabs us. It isn't where we go searching for a passage of Scripture that fits our situation and then use it as God's will. God leads and directs us to this passage as He quietly speaks to our heart.

God wants us to pray His Scriptures, but we have to be careful that we don't take every scripture as a *rhema*, a specific word from God that means this scripture is His will in every situation. Let's look at an example of just claiming a verse in prayer, not knowing if it is God's will in that situation. Say we have a sick friend, so we claim James 5:14-15 which says:

> *Is anyone among you sick? Then he must call for the elders of the church and they are to pray over him, anointing him with oil in the name of the Lord; and the prayer offered in faith will restore the one who is sick, and the Lord will raise him up, and if he has committed sins, they will be forgiven him.*

HOW is the prayer offered to restore the one who is sick?

_____

That means that God has confirmed to you that it is His will to heal this person. If you pray these verses, will God heal your friend? Yes, if it is His will. The key is knowing if it is God's will. Are there times when someone prays but God doesn't heal the person?

Look up and read 2 Corinthians 12:7-9.

2 Corinthians 12:7 WHAT did God give Paul to keep him

from exalting himself? A _____ in the flesh

2 Corinthians 12:8 WHAT did Paul ask the Lord?

_____

Was Paul persistent? HOW many times did he ask? _____

2 Corinthians 12:9 HOW did God respond?

"My _____ is _____ for you, for

power is perfected in _____."

Paul prayed three times for God to heal him but God answered him and told him No. God did not heal Paul because He had a purpose in giving Paul this thorn in the flesh. It was to keep him from exalting himself.

God does not always heal people we pray for because it isn't always His

will. Sometimes God has another purpose for the sickness. We can't use these verses in James as a cure-all anytime we know someone who is sick. We have to be sure when we think we have a *rhema* from God that He has directed us to these verses and it is His will.

Now does this mean that you must always have a *rhema* before you can know God's will? No! Sometimes when you are spending time abiding in God, knowing WHO He is and what His Word says, you will automatically know His will just because you know Him.

But WHAT if God doesn't give us a specific passage, a *rhema,* and even though we are abiding in Him and studying His Word, we don't know what His will is in a certain situation, such as someone being sick? Do we still pray when we don't know what God's will is? Yes. Remember what we learned about the Holy Spirit who helps us in our weakness and intercedes for us when we don't know how to pray (Romans 8:26-27)?

So HOW do we pray when we don't know His will? Pray:

> *Father, I am not sure how to pray in this situation (tell God what the situation is, such as, "My friend has cancer"), and I want my friend to be healed. But most importantly, I want Your will for my friend. I lay down my desires for Yours. Please do what You know is best for my friend. Please heal her if it is Your will, but if it isn't, use this situation for Your glory. Thank You for hearing and answering my prayer according to Your holy will. I ask these things in Jesus' name. Amen.*

WHAT is our safeguard to make sure God and His Spirit are leading us as we search for His will? Let's read Luke 10:38-42 printed out below:

> **38** Now as they were traveling along, He entered a village; and a woman named Martha welcomed Him into her home. **39** She had a sister called Mary, who

was seated at the Lord's feet, listening to His word.
40 But Martha was distracted with all her prepara-
tions; and she came up to Him and said, "Lord, do
You not care that my sister has left me to do all the
serving alone? Then tell her to help me." **41** But the
Lord answered and said to her, "Martha, Martha,
you are worried and bothered about so many things;
42 but only one thing is necessary, for Mary has chosen the good part, which shall not be taken away
from her."

Luke 10:39 WHAT was Mary doing?

_____

Luke 10:40 WHAT was Martha doing?

She was _____ with all her _____.

WHAT did Martha tell the Lord to tell Mary?

_____

Luke 10:41-42 HOW did the Lord answer her?

_____

_____

Luke 10:42 WHO had chosen the only thing that was necessary?

_____

WHAT was that one thing? WHAT was Mary doing?

_____

Did you notice how Martha was worried and distracted? Are you like Martha, or are you like Mary? Do you know WHAT the most important thing is? WHAT did Mary do? She sat at the Lord's feet and listened to Him. Our safeguard to know if God is leading us is to sit at His feet and listen.

So, soldiers, let's do a communication check to make sure those lines of communication are open. Let's review what we have discovered about praying and knowing God's will:

1. We need to surrender by presenting ourselves to God as a living sacrifice. We must give ourselves completely to God. All we want is His will.

2. We need to know God and His Word, to abide in Him.

3. We need to cry out to God. We can ask Him what His will is in a specific situation, and His Spirit may lead us to a specific passage of Scripture (a *rhema*) to show us His will. We have to sit at His feet, listen, and wait.

Fantastic job at cutting and stringing those antennas, soldiers. the Commander in Chief's message was loud and clear!

SCOPING TARGETS UNDER THE COVER OF DARKNESS

Now that you are a pro at being a "shade-tree" radio operator, it's time to do some nighttime work in the field. Special Forces soldiers need to be able to move out at any hour of the day or night. Working under the cover of night gives them an advantage because it allows the element of surprise.

So put on those NVGs (your night vision goggles) and get your orders from the Commander in Chief. Now scope out your first target under the cover of darkness as you begin your maneuvers in the field.

We have spotted our first target. WHERE does intercession fit into Jesus' perfect code on prayer? Do you know what intercession is? That means to pray for someone else. Last week we saw that the Holy Spirit intercedes for us by going to God on our behalf. Surely God wants us to pray for one another, so WHERE do we find intercession in the Lord's Prayer?

Turn to your Observation Worksheet on Matthew 6 on page 153. Read Matthew 6:9-13 and mark the plural personal pronouns *we,* and *our*. Also mark every use of *us* by coloring all of these blue.

Now WHAT did you see? WHOSE Father do we pray to?

_ _ _ Father

Does this prayer say give *me* or give *us* our daily bread?

_____

WHO is to forgive and be forgiven, "me" or "us"?_____

Great shot—you just hit your first target! Jesus uses plural pronouns in His code on prayer because we are not to pray only for ourselves, but we are to pray for others, too!

As you scope out your next target, do you know which sentence in Jesus' code reminds us to pray for those who are lost, those who haven't received Jesus Christ as their Savior yet? Look at the second sentence: "Your kingdom come." As we pray "Your kingdom come," giving our loyalty and our allegiance to the Commander in Chief, we are also praying for Jesus to come back and set His kingdom up on earth.

WHY do you think God hasn't sent Jesus back to rule and reign on the earth yet? Look up and read 2 Peter 3:9. This verse is speaking of Jesus' promise to come back and rule on earth.

WHAT is the Lord waiting for?

_____

Isn't that amazing? God created each and every person on this earth. As we have seen from studying His will, it is His will that all people come to know Him by believing in His Son Jesus so that they can spend eternity with Him. God will not send Jesus back to the earth to set up His kingdom until every person WHO will accept Jesus Christ as his or her Savior believes and becomes a Christian.

So WHAT should you pray for as you pray for God to have first place in your life and for the coming of His kingdom?

_____

Did you hit the second target? Did you write down those who are lost and need a Savior? As we pray using Jesus' special code, the sentence "Your kingdom come" should also remind us to pray for those who need to be saved so that He can return to earth to rule and reign.

Do you know someone who isn't a Christian? Write that person's name and the names of any other people you know who are not saved, as well as any family members, in your logbook on the page titled "Your Kingdom Come." If you have a picture of them, glue it on that page to look at as you lift them up in prayer. Do you know WHAT to pray for them, WHAT to ask God to do? Look at Acts 26:18 printed out below:

> *To open their eyes so that they may turn from darkness to light and from the dominion of Satan to God, that they may receive forgiveness of sins and an inheritance among those who have been sanctified by faith.*

Then pray this as a prayer for your lost friend. Great work, soldier! Even under the cover of darkness you hit the targets to bring about God's kingdom on earth.

4

OPERATION REQUISITION— ASKING AND RECEIVING FROM THE COMMANDER

All right, soldiers! You are on the homestretch of God's "Q" course! As you head into Phase III, there is only one more week of training. Then you will be a member of God's Special Forces, a part of His special A team. Are you ready to get started? Then grab your gear as we check in with the Commander in Chief.

PHASE III

We're good to go, soldier. Are you ready to begin the advanced training portion of God's "Q" course? This final phase will send you back into the field with the members of your unit on an actual simulated field mission to see how you operate under pressure and discover if you have the "right stuff" to wear the GSF beret.

While you wait to be processed and issued your equipment, refresh yourself on Jesus' special code on prayer. WHAT is next? WHAT is the fourth sentence in the Lord's prayer? Write it out on the lines on the next page.

_____ _____ _____ _____ _____

_____ _____.

Now take a look at the scriptures that are printed out below and find the key word that is repeated in all five passages of Scripture. Mark this key word by coloring it **yellow** in each passage of Scripture.

John 14:13—*Whatever you ask in My name, that will I do, so that the Father may be glorified in the Son.*

John 16:23—*In that day you will not question Me about anything. Truly, truly, I say to you, if you ask the Father for anything in My name, He will give it to you.*

Luke 11:9-10—*So I say to you, ask, and it will be given to you; seek, and you will find; knock, and it will be opened to you. For everyone who asks, receives; and he who seeks, finds; and to him who knocks, it will be opened.*

Matthew 21:22—*And all things you ask in prayer, believing, you will receive.*

John 15:16—*You did not choose Me but I chose you, and appointed you that you would go and bear fruit, and that your fruit would remain, so that whatever you ask of the Father in My name He may give to you.*

WHAT is the key word in all these passages? _____

Do we see *asking* in this fourth sentence in the Lord's Prayer? _____Yes _____ No

WHAT title did we give this sentence?

_____

Do you know WHAT *petition* means? *Petition* means "to ask or to make a request." So WHAT is Jesus' teaching us to pray about in this sentence? He wants us to ask for WHAT?

_____

HOW are we to ask? Look back at the passages of Scripture on John 14:13; 16:23; and 15:16 to find out HOW we are to ask.

In _____   _____

WHOSE name is this? Do you know?

___ ___ ___ ___ ___

These scriptures show us that we are to come to the Father in prayer and ask for our requests in Jesus' name. That doesn't just mean we throw in Jesus' name as we pray. It means that we ask according to His character and His ways. We pray to the Father through the Son according to WHO He is, according to God's Word.

Now do we ask just one time, or do we keep on asking? Do you remember what you learned about asking in Week One in Luke 11:9-10? This verb *asks* is in the present tense, which means it is a continuous action. Remember, we are to keep on asking; we are to be persistent in prayer.

Now take a look at James 4:1-3 printed out below:

1 What is the source of quarrels and conflicts among you? Is not the source your pleasures that wage war in your members? **2** You lust and do not have; so you commit murder. You are envious and cannot obtain; so you fight and quarrel. You do not have because you do not ask. **3** You ask and do not receive, because you ask with wrong motives, so that you may spend it on your pleasures.

James 4:2 WHY are they fighting and quarreling?

_____

WHY don't they have?

_____

So HOW are we to have? We are to _____.

Are they trusting in God, since they did not ask? _____

James 4:3 WHY don't they receive what they asked for?

_____

So does it matter HOW we ask? _____ Yes _____ No

Remember, God always does what is best for us. So when we ask for the wrong reasons, God will say no to our requests.

Let's compare this passage in James with Isaiah 31:1 printed out below:

> _Woe to those who go down to Egypt for help and rely on horses, and trust in chariots because they are many and in horsemen because they are very strong, but they do not look to the Holy One of Israel, nor seek the LORD!_

WHERE did they go for help?

_____

WHAT did they trust in?

_____

WHOM did they not look to or seek?

_____

WHAT was the result? ____ ____ ____ to those

Both James and Isaiah show us that we are to seek God for the things that we need. We are not to place our trust in ourselves or in the world. Did you know that Egypt is a picture of the world? God is our Provider. We are to place our trust in Him.

- Now, in WHOM do you place your trust: God or man?

_____

- Do you ask God for the things that you need, or do you try to do it all by yourself?

_____

As you finish your processing, get in some prayer practice. Title the next page in your logbook "Give Us This Day Our Daily Bread, Petition and Intercession." Decorate this page and write out a prayer to the Commander in Chief, asking Him to meet your needs. Tell Him that you want to trust and depend on Him for all your needs.

REQUISITIONING SUPPLIES

All right, soldiers, now that you have been processed and issued your equipment, it's time for refresher training on helicopter and parachute procedures. We need to plan our air and parachute operations so that we are ready for our simulated field mission.

As we carefully plan this operation, we also need to make sure we have enough supplies for our mission and that we know the exact location of our DZ (drop zone). We need a clear area where we can drop our supplies safely without the enemy's interference. Our enemy's primary task in this field exercise is to cut off our supplies so that our mission will be unsuccessful.

Let's take a look at our training manuals to study the exact procedure for requisitioning and receiving our supplies. WHAT does God's Word show us in James 1:17 printed out below?

> *Every good thing given and every perfect gift is from above, coming down from the Father of lights, with whom there is no variation or shifting shadow.*

WHO is the giver? _____

WHAT does He give?

_____

Now look at the promise God has given us in Philippians 4:19:

> *And my God will supply all your needs according to His riches in glory in Christ Jesus.*

WHAT will God do?

_____

HOW? according to His _____

Wow! Our Commander in Chief has all the supplies that we will ever need waiting just for us. He is our Supplier. Do you remember what we saw yesterday as we looked at Isaiah 31:1? We saw that when we try to do things without the help of God by putting our trust in the world and in ourselves, the result is woe! We will live a life of woe, a life that is cursed.

Now let's look at Jeremiah 17:5-8 printed out below and mark the following key words:

cursed (draw a box in orange and color it brown)

blessed (draw a blue cloud around it and color it pink)

> **5** Thus says the LORD, "Cursed is the man who trusts in mankind and makes flesh his strength, and whose heart turns away from the LORD. **6** For he will be like a bush in the desert and will not see when prosperity comes, but will live in stony wastes in the wilderness, a land of salt without inhabitant. **7** Blessed is the man who trusts in the LORD and whose trust is the LORD. **8** For he will be like a tree planted by the water, that extends its roots by a stream and will not fear when the heat comes; but its leaves will be green, and it will not be anxious in a year of drought nor cease to yield fruit.

Now ask the 5 W's and an H to solve the crossword puzzle and see the results of where we place our trust.

Jeremiah 17:5 WHY is the man cursed? WHO does he place his trust in?

1. (Down) in _____

WHAT does he make his strength?

2. (Across) _____

Jeremiah 17:6 WHAT will this cursed man be like?

3. (Down) a _____ in the 4. (Down)_____

He will live in stony wastes in the

5. (Down) _____

Jeremiah 17:7 WHY is this man blessed?

6. (Down) He _____ in the Lord.

Jeremiah 17:8 WHAT will the blessed man be like?

7. (Across) a _____ planted by the

8. (Down) _____, that extends its

9. (Across)_____ by a 10. (Across) _____

and will not 11. (Across) _____ when the

12. (Down) _____ comes; but its 13. (Across)_____

will be 14. (Across) _____, and

it will not be 15. (Across) _____ in a year of

16. (Across) _____ nor cease to yield

17. (Down) _____.

Draw a picture in the boxes below so that you can see with your own eyes the contrasts, the differences in these two men. In the first box draw the description of the cursed man, and in the second box draw a picture that describes the blessed man.

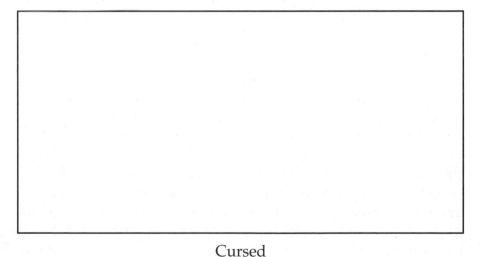

Cursed

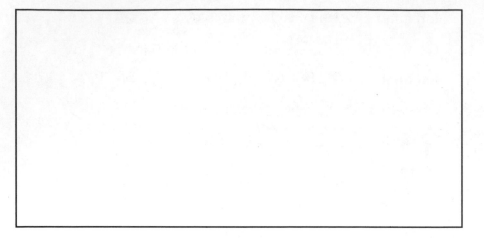

Blessed

WHAT a difference in these two men! WHICH one do you want to be like: the one whose trust is in himself and is cursed, or the one whose trust is in the Lord and is blessed?

_____

Are you anxious in hard times (times of heat)? Or are you resting because you know that the heat can't destroy you because you are rooted by a stream and God will meet your needs? Write out which one is a picture of you.

_____

   HOW dependent are you on God? Have you sent your requisition (inquiry) to the Commander in Chief asking for the supplies for your mission? Communicate with Him and ask Him to supply your needs from His riches, to make you like the tree that is planted by the water, so that even in times of drought when there is no rain (hard times) you will not be anxious. Thank Him for His provision and that, like the tree by a stream, you will yield fruit because your supplies come straight from Him.

COMMUNiCATiON WiTH THE COMMANDER

"Prayer Warrior 1, this is Chief. Over."

"Chief, this is Prayer Warrior 1. Over."

"Prayer Warrior 1, this is Chief. Are supplies ready and Delta Zula located? Over."

"Chief, this is Prayer Warrior 1. Supplies are ready and Delta Zula located. Over."

"Prayer Warrior 1, this is Chief. Roger. Execute mission. Over."

"Chief, this is Prayer Warrior 1. Wilco. Out."

Your communication was loud and clear, soldier. Now let's take another look at this fourth sentence in our prayer code.

WHAT are we to ask God to give us?

_____

WHAT do you think Jesus means when He tells us to pray for our bread? Are we to ask only for food? _____ Yes _____ No

No. Jesus uses the word *bread* because it represents all that we need to live our lives.

WHAT was this bread called? ___ ___ ___ ___ ___ (aidyl)

God's name is Jehovah Jireh. He is our Provider. This means we are to come to God and ask Him to meet our needs each and every day.

Look up and read 1 Thessalonians 5:17.

HOW are we to pray?

_____

We are to be in constant communication with our Commander in Chief as we go about our daily lives. We are to live our lives in the attitude of prayer. We are to pray without ceasing as we continually walk with Him.

Now HOW do we ask? Review WHAT you learned, soldier, from the third sentence of Jesus' code on prayer:

We are to ask according to _____ _____.

HOW do we seek His will? We are to ___ ___ ___ ___ ___

in Him and have His words ___ ___ ___ ___ ___ in us.

Unscramble the word in the parentheses if you don't remember the word that goes in these blanks (diabe).

WHAT do we do? We are surrendered and abiding. HOW do we communicate so that God will grant our request?

Read 2 Corinthians 1:20 printed out below:

> *For as many as are the promises of God, in Him*
> *they are yes; therefore also through Him is our*
> *Amen to the glory of God through us.*

WHAT are we to plead? HOW do we get our yes?

the _____ of _____

HOW do we pray the promises of God? WHAT have we seen over and over as we have learned about praying? WHAT do we have to study so that we will know WHO God is? HOW do we abide in Him?

by knowing His ____ ____ ___ ___ (orwd)

That's the key to asking, soldier. HOW can we plead God's promises if we don't know His Word? The Bible is your very own prayer book. As you study God's Word and learn His promises, you will know exactly HOW to pray your requests. Let's take a look at Moses and see HOW he pleaded God's promises in prayer.

Read Exodus 32:9-14 printed out below:

> **9** The LORD said to Moses, "I have seen this people, and behold, they are an obstinate people. **10** Now then let Me alone, that My anger may burn against them and that I may destroy them; and I will make of you a great nation." **11** Then Moses entreated the LORD his God, and said, "O LORD, why does Your anger burn against Your people whom You have brought out from the land of Egypt with great power and with a mighty hand? **12** Why should the Egyptians speak, saying, 'With evil intent He brought them out to kill them in the mountains and to destroy them from the face of the earth'? Turn from Your burning anger and change Your mind about doing harm to Your people. **13** Remember Abraham, Isaac, and Israel, Your servants to whom You swore by Yourself, and said to them, 'I will multiply your descendants as the stars of the heavens, and all this land of which I have spoken I will give to your descendants, and they shall inherit it forever.' " **14** So the LORD changed His mind about the harm which He said He would do to His people.

Exodus 32:9-11 WHY did Moses go to the Lord in prayer? WHAT was God going to do to the children of Israel?

_____

Exodus 32:11 HOW does Moses begin his prayer?

_____

Exodus 32:9-13 Does Moses want God to destroy His

people and make him a great nation? _____

Exodus 32:12 WHAT does Moses ask God to do?

_____

_____

Exodus 32:13 WHAT does Moses ask God to remember?

_____

WHAT promise did God give to Abraham, Isaac, and
Israel?

_____

_____

Exodus 32:14 WHAT is the result of Moses reminding
God of His promise?

_____

Amazing! Do you see HOW very powerful prayer is? Moses
goes to God and reminds Him of His promise to Abraham,
Isaac, and Israel. God not only hears Moses' prayer, but He
also changes His mind and does not harm His people. WHAT
an awesome privilege to be able to communicate with God,
asking for His help as you plead the promises in His Word.

Let's practice praying God's Word. HOW can we pray if we
are afraid? Let's look at Isaiah 41:13:

> *For I am the* L<small>ORD</small> *your God, who upholds your right hand, who says to you, "Do not fear, I will help you."*

Now, let's claim this promise in prayer:

> *Heavenly Father, I praise You because You alone are God! I know that I am not alone in this situation. You are right here with me, holding my right hand! Please help me to remember Your promise in Isaiah 41:13. You said I am not to fear. You will help me. I am trusting You, Lord. I give You my fear and ask that You take care of this situation. I give You all the thanks and all the glory. I ask this in Your Son Jesus' name, my great High Priest who intercedes for me (Hebrews 7:25). Amen.*

PACKING THE SUPPLIES

Okay, soldier, our supplies are ready and waiting for us at the command post. Before we pick them up and load the helicopter, we need to go over our supply list. Part of this mission is to not only know what we need to pack for our part in this special "op" but to also know what to pack for the other members in our unit. Our goal is to make sure every member has just the right equipment. So check in with the Commander in Chief and pull out those training manuals.

So far we have been focusing on asking God for our needs as we have looked at the fourth sentence in the Lord's Prayer. But remember, there is an *us* and this *us* isn't just for us personally, but to remind us to pray for others, too!

Look up and read 1 Timothy 2:1-6.

WHOM are we to pray for?

We are to pray on behalf of _____ _____, for

_____ and all who are in _____.

The first thing we see is that we are to pray on the behalf of all men. Pull out your logbook and under "Give Us This Day Our Daily Bread, Petition and Intercession" write out the names of the people that you want to pray for: parents, friends, family members, etc. Then, beside their names list their needs.

Remember what we have learned about praying for God's will and what we saw in James 4:1-3 about asking with wrong motives.

Think about WHY you are asking God for this request. WHAT is your motive? Can you ask for it in Jesus' name?

Is it according to His character and His ways? Will it bring Him glory? Remember, your requests need to line up with Him!

If you have any pictures of the people you are praying for, glue these on this logbook page also. And don't forget to add your needs to this list, too!

Then as you pray for each one of these people and see God's answers, write out how He answered your request to remind you of His faithfulness, how He hears and answers our prayers. But be patient! God answers prayers in His own time and according to His will, so don't be disappointed if the answer doesn't come right away.

After you list the people you know, HOW about praying for those you don't know? Remember, we are to pray for all men. HOW about praying for the poor and hungry? Have you ever gone to bed hungry? If you have, you know that it's not a good feeling. Most of us have plenty to eat, but there are kids who go to bed hungry each and every night. Some of these kids may not even have a home where they are safe and warm.

Remember, you are to pray for daily needs. So as you sit down to eat your dinner, pray for those who don't have anything to eat. As you crawl into your nice warm bed, pray for those kids who may be living on the streets. And as you play out in your yard, remember that not all neighborhoods are safe places to play. Some are filled with violence, crime, and drugs. Pray that God will clean up those neighborhoods and provide a safe place for those kids to live and play.

First Timothy 2:1-6 also shows us that we are to pray for those in authority. WHO are these people? HOW about the president of the United States, our elected officials, the judges of our country, as well as the military who defend and protect our country? HOW about the other nations around the world and their leaders? HOW about your pastor, your church, missionaries, your teachers, your principal, and leaders of the community? All of these people are in positions of authority and leadership and need your prayers.

You might want to write all these names in your logbook and focus on praying for different groups of people on a certain day of the week.

But HOW do you know WHAT to pray for? We have given you some ideas below to help you as you learn how to pray for each group of people. Don't forget: If you have any pictures of these people, glue these pictures in your logbook. You might want to draw a picture of our nation's flag, your school, church, etc., to give you a visual as you pray for those particular people each day.

Sunday: The president of the United States

Glue a picture of the president on this page or draw the flag of the USA. Read the newspaper and watch the news to find out what decisions our president needs to make so that you can pray for those decisions.

Ask God to protect the president of the United States and keep him from all harm. Ask God to give him strength when

he is tired, to give him wisdom to know
and do the right thing for our country.
Ask God to give us a godly president
who seeks God's will, instead of being
conformed to this world. Ask God to
help him be humble and not proud, to let
His Holy Spirit lead and guide him as he
serves our country, to give him the courage to
make godly decisions that truly make our country
one nation under God.

Monday: Elected officials

Find out WHO is your congressman, sena-
tor, and governor and pray for them by name. Ask
God to give all our elected officials the wisdom to know what
is right and the courage to do it. Pray that God will lead them
as they make laws that run our country. Ask Him to help
those who are on opposite sides to be able to work together
and do what is right for the country. Ask God to lead
Christians to run for office so that our country will have godly
leadership.

Tuesday: Judges and justices of the Supreme Court

Ask God to only appoint judges who are righteous, and
who will do what is right in His eyes. Ask God to help them
know His Word so they can make the right decisions for our
country. Pray that He will give them wisdom as they make
life-and-death decisions each day.

Wednesday: The military

Ask God to give our military the ability to defend our country from harm and evil forces. Ask Him to give our military
leaders wisdom as they send our men and women out to protect our country. Ask God to keep each one safe and to put a
hedge of protection around them, to give them strength when
they are tired and comfort them when they are sad and lonely.
Pray for God to give them courage and help them to not be
afraid, and to give them success in their missions as they fight
to keep us safe and protect our freedom.

Thursday: Other nations and their leaders

Glue pictures from magazines of kids from different countries. Then get a world map or a globe and call the nations by name as you pray for them. If you would like to know more information about the nations, like how big they are, you can get the book *Operation World* by Patrick Johnston. Another way to learn about a particular nation is to read a book that is set in that country. A good fictional book series about a boy living in Russia during the time it was a communist country is the Ivan Series written by Myrna Grant. This series of books shows you what it was like to live in a country where worshiping God is forbidden. As you study and learn about different countries, ask God to show you how you should pray.

Pray by asking God to send people to all the nations to teach them about Jesus. Pray that God will get rid of those leaders who persecute and kill, and ask Him to put godly leaders in their place. Ask God to protect the Christians in these nations from being persecuted and tortured, to keep them safe, to bring forth His kingdom on earth.

Friday: Your pastor, church, and missionaries

Draw a picture of your church and glue any prayer cards that you may have of missionaries on this page.

Ask God to give your pastor the time to study God's Word. Pray that God will help him preach straight from the Bible so that others can hear God's Word and know how important it is.

Ask God to give the leaders of your church wisdom as they make decisions. Ask God to bless the church and to help the members minister to those in their community.

Ask God to help the church members get along with each other, like Jesus prayed in John 17 that the believers would be one like He and the Father are one.

Ask God to lead church members to witness to those who aren't saved and to disciple the members who are in the church so that they can grow in their relationship with Him.

Ask God to bless and provide the needs of His missionaries. Ask Him to keep them safe as they work in other cities and nations to teach and show people their need for Him. Pray that God will give them good health and the strength they need to help others and to be the hands of Jesus each and every day.

Saturday: Your teachers, your principal, and community leaders

Draw a picture of your school or community. You might want to get an adult and some friends and do a prayer walk around your school or in your community. As you walk around the school, pray for different teachers, the principal, and for lost and hurting kids.

Ask God to help you be a good witness at school, to care for other people, and to reach out to kids who are left out. Ask God to move in your school and draw the lost to Him. Ask Him to keep ungodly people from pushing their ideas on everyone else.

Ask God to give you godly leadership in your community and schools. Ask Him to move the leaders in our country to change our laws so that prayer is allowed back in our schools.

Ask Him to give the teachers wisdom as they teach and to make learning fun and exciting each day. Ask God to provide protection in our schools, to get rid of all the evil influences, and to keep the kids safe. Ask God to give us strong community leaders who will keep our communities safe by getting rid of drugs and gangs.

Outstanding! You are packed and ready to go, soldier.

OPERATION EAGLE WING

Let's move, soldiers! We have our supplies, the equipment is onboard, and we have the go-ahead from the Commander in Chief. It's time to begin our special "op": Operation Eagle

Wing. Is your parachute ready? Then head to the chopper. The next three days will show the Commander that we have just what it takes to be a part of His Special Forces. Don't forget your prayer cover. Now we're ready. Let's roll!

Let's plan our mission. Take a look at the fifth sentence in the Lord's Prayer: "And forgive us our debts, as we also have forgiven our debtors."

WHAT are we asking God to do in this sentence?

_____

WHAT are our debts? WHAT do we need to be forgiven of?

Our __ __ __

WHY did Jesus wait until this fifth sentence to mention the subject of confession and forgiveness? WHO would our focus be on if we began our prayers by confessing our sins? _____

Because prayer is coming into the presence of an almighty God, our focus should be on Him and not on ourselves. Also, as we focus on God in worship, giving Him our commitment of loyalty, praying for His kingdom, seeking His will, and asking in total dependence for His provision, then we will see where we have fallen. We will see our need for forgiveness.

Let's take a look at our training manuals and gather some information on sin and forgiveness. Read John 1:29 printed out below:

> *The next day he saw Jesus coming to him and said, "Behold, the Lamb of God who takes away the sin of the world!"*

WHO takes away the sins of the world?

_____

Read 2 Corinthians 5:21:

> *He made Him who knew no sin to be sin on our behalf, so that we might become the righteousness of God in Him.*

WHAT was Jesus made on our behalf?

_____

WHY?

_____

Read Hebrews 10:10-12 printed out below:

10 By this will we have been sanctified through the offering of the body of Jesus Christ once for all. **11** Every priest stands daily ministering and offering time after time the same sacrifices, which can never take away sins; **12** but He, having offered one sacrifice for sins for all time, sat down at the right hand of God.

Hebrews 10:10 HOW are we sanctified?

_____

Hebrews 10:12 HOW long does that sacrifice last?

_____

So WHY do we need to come to God in prayer after we are saved and ask for forgiveness if Jesus paid the price for all our sins past, present, and future, when He was made to be sin on the cross for us?

When Jesus died on the cross we were sanctified—we were set apart and made right with God once and for all. But even though we are now children of God, we still live in fleshly bodies that continue to sin.

WHAT does sin do to our relationship with God? Let's find out by looking at the following scriptures:

> *Isaiah 59:1-2—Behold, the LORD's hand is not so short that it cannot save; nor is His ear so dull that it cannot hear. But your iniquities have made a separation between you and your God, and your sins have hidden His face from you so that He does not hear.*

WHAT do our iniquities (our sins) do?

_____

Does God hear? ____ Yes ____ No

> *Psalm 66:18—If I regard wickedness in my heart, the Lord will not hear.*

WHAT happens when there is wickedness in our heart?

_____

> *Proverbs 28:9—He who turns away his ear from listening to the law, even his prayer is an abomination.*

WHEN we don't listen, WHAT is our prayer?

_____

Proverbs 28:13—He who conceals his transgressions will not prosper, but he who confesses and forsakes them will find compassion.

WHAT happens to the one who conceals his transgression (his sin)?

_____

WHAT happens to the one who confesses and forsakes his sin?

_____

1 Peter 3:12—For the eyes of the Lord are toward the righteous, and His ears attend to their prayer, but the face of the Lord is against those who do evil.

WHAT does God do for the righteous (those who have been made right with God and live the way God wants them to live)?

_____

HOW about those who do evil?

_____

Do you see WHY it is important to ask God for forgiveness when we sin, even though Jesus has already paid for those sins? Sin puts a barrier between God and us. It separates us so that God will not hear our prayers. Sin hinders our relationship with God. Our lines of communication are cut off until we make things right with Him.

HOW can we make things right? WHAT are we to do when we sin? Read 1 John 1:9 printed out below:

> *If we confess our sins, He is faithful and righteous to forgive us our sins and to cleanse us from all unrighteousness.*

> WHAT are we to do so that we can be forgiven and made clean again?

_____

After we confess, we are forgiven and cleansed. Communication is restored. Our lines of communication are free and clear and back in order once again.

Look back at the scripture printed out on Proverbs 28:13.

> WHAT happens to the one who confesses and forsakes his sins?

_____

Now look at James 5:16 printed out below:

> *Therefore, confess your sins to one another, and pray for one another so that you may be healed. The effective prayer of a righteous man can accomplish much.*

> WHAT are we to do with one another?

_____

After we confess, WHAT are we to do?

_____

If we go to other Christians and tell them what we did wrong, then they can pray for us, too!

> WHAT do we learn about the prayer of a righteous man (a man who has been made right with God and lives the way God wants him to live)?

_____

> Did we see a man like that in Week One? WHO prayed the heavens open and shut? If you don't remember, look up James 5:17 for the answer.

_____

Now that you have seen just how sin affects our prayer life, you know why Jesus gave us these instructions of asking for forgiveness in His special code on prayer. Pull out your logbooks and title the next page in your log book "Confession and Forgiveness," then record Psalm 51:10 printed out below:

> *Create in me a clean heart, O God, and renew a steadfast spirit within me.*

This is a part of David's prayer that he prayed after Nathan had confronted him about his sin with Bathsheba, a woman he loved who wasn't his wife.

Now pray this prayer, confess your sins to your Father, and receive His cleansing and His forgiveness so that the lines of communication are free and clear once again.

MAKING THE JUMP

Okay, soldiers, we should be over the DZ at 2100 hours. After we drop the supplies and equipment, we will head to our landing area to make our jump. As we hit the ground, the first order of business is a tactical move off the landing zone. We need to assemble at our rallying point to get a head count and align ourselves as we begin Operation Eagle Wing.

Is everyone in position? Good. We have received the all clear.

Yesterday we spent the day looking at "And forgive us our debts," the first half of the fifth sentence in Jesus' prayer code. We saw how sin separates us from God and how important it is to ask for forgiveness. But what about the second part of this sentence: "as we also have forgiven our debtors"? WHAT does this mean? Do we have to forgive those who have sinned against and hurt us? Let's find out.

Turn to your Observation Worksheet on page 168 and read Matthew 18:21-35. Mark the key word *forgive* *(forgave)* by circling it in red.

Now continue your mission, asking the 5 W's and an H.

Matthew 18:21 WHO comes to Jesus to ask Him about forgiving his brother?

_____

HOW many times did Peter think he should forgive his brother?

_____

Matthew 18:22 WHAT was Jesus' response? HOW many times was he to forgive?

_____

After Jesus answers Peter's questions, He tells him a parable. A parable is a story that teaches a moral lesson or truth. Although the story is not usually a real story, it is a story that is true-to-life. A parable is designed to make one main point, and Jesus uses this parable to teach Peter about forgiveness.

WHAT happens in this parable? Let's find out.

Matthew 18:23-24 HOW much did the slave owe his king?

_____

Matthew 18:25 Could the slave repay what he owed? ___

Matthew 18:27 WHAT did the king feel and WHAT did he do for the slave?

_____

Matthew 18:28 Now WHAT does the slave do?

_____

HOW much did his fellow slave owe him?

_____

Matthew 18:30 WHAT did he do to his fellow slave?

_____

Matthew 18:31 WHAT did the other slaves do?

_____

Matthew 18:32-34 WHAT did the king do to this slave because the slave did not have mercy on his fellow slave?

_____

_____

Wow! Jesus tells Peter this story to show him how gracious and merciful the king was to forgive this slave who owed 10,000 talents, which would be around ten million dollars, and yet this slave would not forgive his fellow slave who owed him only 100 denarii, about a day's wage.

Because of this slave's lack of mercy and unforgiving heart, he was handed over to the torturers until he could repay his debt. Do you want to end up like that slave? Look at the last verse—Matthew 18:35.

WHAT will God do to us if we do not forgive our brother from our heart?

_____

So is it important for us to forgive those who have done the wrong thing to us? ____ Yes ____ No

Let's look at some cross-references to see what God's Word has to say about forgiveness.

Matthew 6:14-15 WHAT happens if we forgive other people for their transgressions?

_____

WHAT happens if we don't forgive?

_____

Look up and read Colossians 2:13-14.

WHAT did Jesus do when we were dead in our transgressions?

_____

Colossians 2:14 WHAT did He cancel out?

_____

Look up and read Colossians 3:12-13.

HOW are those who are chosen of God to behave?

_____

_____

Look up and read Ephesians 4:32. HOW are we to treat one another?

_____

_____

WHY?

_____

Do you see how important forgiveness is? God's Word shows us very clearly that we are to forgive because Jesus has forgiven us. If we don't forgive others, then Jesus won't forgive us (Matthew 6:14-15).

Forgiving someone doesn't mean that you will be able to forget what happened, and it doesn't mean that the person who wronged you won't be punished. It means that you are handing what they did to you over to God, and that you will let God be their Judge. You will not hold their offense against them. You will let it go; you will set them free.

Now pull out your logbook and turn to the page titled "Confession and Forgiveness" and write out "I need to forgive (put down the person's name that you need to forgive) because he (tell what the person did to you).

Then go to God and tell Him whom you need to forgive and why. Tell Him that you can't do it, but you know He can do it through you. Turn your hurt and anger over to Him. Remember, God is in control and He will use this for your good. Trust God and lean on His promise in Romans 8:28:

> *And we know that God causes all things to work together for good to those who love God, to those who are called according to His purpose.*

Now, God didn't say that all things are good, but that He causes all things to work for good. Pray and ask God to use the things that have hurt you for good because you love Him.

KEEPING WATCH—UNDER THE EAGLE'S WING

Let's go, soldiers. Move it, move it, move it! The enemy is right behind us. We need to fan out so that we can avoid being captured. Put a call in to the Commander in Chief for prayer cover and head for safety. Once we are squared away and have set up our watch post, we will send out a patrol while we hold our position.

Take a look at the sixth sentence in Jesus' code on prayer: "And do not lead us into temptation, but deliver us from evil." Would our Commander in Chief lead us into temptation and put us in a position to be captured by our enemy?

Take a look at James 1:13-14 printed out below:

> *Let no one say when he is tempted, "I am being tempted by God"; for God cannot be tempted by evil, and He Himself does not tempt anyone. But each one is tempted when he is carried away and enticed by his own lust.*

Does God tempt anyone? _____

HOW are we tempted?

_____

WHY would Jesus tell us to pray "And do not lead us into temptation, but deliver us from evil" if James tells us God does not tempt anyone? Do these two passages contradict each other? No! Remember our very important rule: Scripture never contradicts Scripture.

So what does this verse mean, "lead us not into temptation"? Jesus is calling us to vigilance. He is telling us to keep watch. This sentence is a "preventive" prayer; it's like planning ahead and packing your supplies so that you are prepared before you are called to move out.

Then if you receive the orders to go, you are prepared and ready. By praying this sixth sentence, you are telling God, "I want to do the right thing, Lord. Help me not to fail." You want to make sure that when temptation comes, you can handle the temptation without falling into sin.

Let's turn to our Observation Worksheet on page 171 and read Matthew 26:36-44. Be vigilant. Ask the 5 W's and an H.

Matthew 26:36 WHAT is Jesus going to do? _____

Matthew 26:38 WHAT does Jesus ask Peter and the two sons of Zebedee to do?

_____

Matthew 26:40 WHAT are the disciples doing?

_____

Are they keeping watch? ____ Yes ____ No

Matthew 26:41 HOW do you keep from entering into temptation?

_____

_____

WHY are you to keep watch?

_____

_____

   Jesus gives us this sixth sentence in His special prayer code because even though we love God and want to follow Him, we are made of flesh and our flesh is weak. We are to keep on watching and keep on praying so that we don't give in to our flesh and sin.

• Are you watching? Are you being careful where you go, what you see, what you think, what you listen to, and what you do? _____ Yes _____ No

Matthew 26:33 WHAT did Peter tell Jesus he would never do?

_____

_____

Matthew 26:34 WHAT did Jesus tell Peter he would do?

_____

_____

Matthew 26:69-75 WHAT happened to Peter, who slept instead of keeping watch?

_____

Now take at look at the passage in Luke 22:31-34 printed out below.

> **31** "Simon, Simon, behold, Satan has demanded permission to sift you like wheat; **32** but I have prayed for you, that your faith may not fail; and you, when once you have turned again, strengthen your brothers." **33** But he said to Him, "Lord, with You I am ready to go both to prison and to death!" **34** And He said, "I say to you, Peter, the rooster will not crow today until you have denied three times that you know Me."

Luke 22:31 WHAT does Satan demand permission to do?

_____

Luke 22:32 HOW does Jesus pray?

_____

As Satan demands to test Peter, Jesus knows that even though Peter is willing, his flesh is weak and he will fail this test. So HOW does He pray for Peter? Jesus prays that Peter's faith may not fail—that after Peter falls, he will turn again and strengthen his brothers.

Did this happen? Yes, Peter denied Jesus, but he turned back to Jesus and was restored. If you study John 21, you will see how Jesus called Peter to tend His sheep even after he failed to follow Him.

Look at 1 Peter 5:8 printed out below:

> *Be of sober spirit, be on the alert. Your adversary, the devil, prowls around like a roaring lion, seeking someone to devour.*

WHO is prowling like a lion? _____

WHAT are we to do?

_____

Satan is looking to devour us, but Jesus has shown us in His prayer that we are to keep watch. We are to pray and ask God to keep us from falling into temptation. This sentence reminds us to be on the alert!

Now can we do it? Can we keep from falling? Take a look at the promise that God gives us in 1 Corinthians 10:13:

> *No temptation has overtaken you but such as is common to man; and God is faithful, who will not allow you to be tempted beyond what you are able, but with the temptation will provide the way of escape also, so that you will be able to endure it.*

WHAT do we see about God?

_____

WHAT does God promise us about temptations?

No temptation has _____ you.

God will not allow you to be tempted beyond what you

are _____.

God will provide the way of _____ so that you

will be able to _____ it.

God is faithful. He will provide our deliverance. All we have to do is cry out to Him. Don't forget to pray this prayer for other people too. Look at Ephesians 6:18:

> *With all prayer and petition pray at all times in the Spirit, and with this in view, be on the alert with all perseverance and petition for all the saints.*

HOW are we to pray? _____

WHAT are we to do?

_____

_____

WHO are we to petition for? _____

Way to go! Now get out your logbook and title the next page "God's Deliverance from Temptation and Evil." Draw a picture of soldiers on the alert, keeping watch. Also write any names of people that you would like to pray for. Maybe you have a Christian friend who is being tempted to look at things he shouldn't look at. Maybe he is doing something that you know is wrong. Ask God to keep him from falling into temptation:

> *God, You are a faithful God. You are my Deliverer. Please help me to keep watch for the things that might cause me to sin. Help me not to do the things I know are wrong. Help me to obey Your Word. Help me to stay away from wrong friends and wrong places so I won't be tempted to do the wrong thing.*
>
> *Please help my friend (call him by name), who is being tempted to do (name whatever it is). Please keep him from acting on this temptation. Help me to remember Your promise in 1 Corinthians 10:13 that no temptation can overtake me. You will provide a way of escape. I thank You for hearing my prayer. I ask these things in Jesus' name, knowing that even though He was tempted, He did not fall. Amen.*

All right! Operation Eagle Wing is complete! As we occupy the territory, let's look at the last sentence in our special coded prayer: "For Yours is the kingdom and the power and the glory forever. Amen."

WHAT is this? _____

Worship. As we come to the last sentence in Jesus' prayer, this sentence is like the hallelujah chorus. Isn't it incredible? It is our triumph in Christ Jesus! Forever and ever all the power and glory are His! Sing cadences to the Commander in Chief! Praise Him for being all-powerful. There is no one else like Him, and He will rule forever and ever! Amen! Let me hear it, GSF, as we march back to the barracks:

God is good, and God is great,
He can make the nations quake!
Sound off, 1, 2
Sound off, 3, 4
He is strong and full of might,
My Deliverer day or night.
Sound off, 1, 2
Sound off, 3, 4
I will give Him first and best.
He is God I'll do no less.
Sound off, 1, 2
Sound off, 3, 4
I will come and I will ask.
Persistence will be my task.
Sound off, 1, 2
Sound off, 3, 4
He loves us, so we love Him,
Sent His Son to deliver us from sin!
Sound off, 1, 2
Sound off, 3, 4
He will rule, and He will reign,

Glory and power to His name.
Sound off, 1, 2
Sound off, 3, 4
Sing it loud, and sing it strong,
Sing God's praises all day long!

Way to go! Aren't you excited, soldier? Even though you are hot, tired, and dirty, you have successfully completed your mission. After spending 28 days on God's "Q" course you know how to pray!

Hit the showers and get dressed for your very special awards dinner at 1800 hours. Way to go, soldier. Operation Prayer was a success!

SPECIAL OPERATION PRAYER—MISSION COMPLETE!

You did it, soldier! You completed God's "Q" course. You are now a member of God's Special Forces. You have earned the right to wear the GSF beret! All right! We are so very proud of you!

The award ceremony is about to begin. Stand up tall as Captain Bryant presents you with your GSF beret and your patch that shows your first official assignment as a GSF soldier. Congratulations, soldier. You have stood firm, you have passed the test!

Just look at all you have discovered about being a communications specialist with the Commander in Chief. You know how to come into

His presence, how to honor and reverence Him. You know your loyalty and devotion belong to Him, that you are to pray for His kingdom and those who are lost, that you are to surrender to Him and give Him control of your life.

You know that He is your Provider, that you are to be totally dependent on Him. He will supply all your needs, as well as the needs of other people. You have seen that sin separates you from the Commander in Chief and that you need to confess your sins, and ask for forgiveness, as well as forgive those who have hurt you.

In Operation Eagle Wing you saw the Commander in Chief deliver you from the hands of the enemy. As you worked in your training manual, you saw you are to ask all these things according to His will, in His Son Jesus' name. You have seen just how powerful and awesome the Commander in Chief is and how much He loves you and wants you on His special A team.

Don't forget to go to www.precept.org/D4Ycertificate to print your special certificate for persevering until the end! We hate to see you leave Camp MacHaven, but our Commander in Chief needs you out on the battlefield.

So pack up your gear, and don't forget your training manual. Knowing God's Word is the key to Operation Prayer. Keep your SATCOM on and those lines of communication open as you begin your life of service with the Commander in Chief.

Dismissed, soldier. See you out in the field.

In His Service,

Captain Bryant

Captain Bryant
God's Special Forces

Pages 28-29

W O R S H I P
"Your kingdom come."

A L L E G I A N C E
"Your will be done, on earth as it is in heaven."

S U B M I S S I O N
"Give us this day our daily bread."

P E T I T I O N   and

I N T E R C E S S I O N
"And forgive us our debts, as we also have forgiven our debtors."

C O N F E S S I O N   and

F O R G I V E N E S S
"And do not lead us into temptation, but deliver us from evil."

D E L I V E R A N C E
"For Yours is the kingdom and the power and the glory forever. Amen."

W O R S H I P

Page 44

Page 72

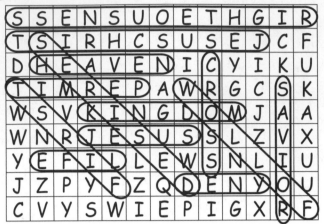

Page 82

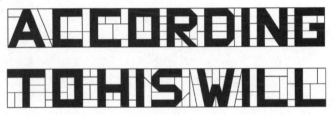

ACCORDING TO HIS WILL

Page 114

TRAINING MANUAL
OBSERVATION WORKSHEETS

Luke 11

1 It happened that while Jesus was praying in a certain place, after He had finished, one of His disciples said to Him, "Lord, teach us to pray just as John also taught his disciples."

2 And He said to them, "When you pray, say: 'Father, hallowed be Your name. Your kingdom come.

3 'Give us each day our daily bread.

4 'And forgive us our sins, For we ourselves also forgive every one who is indebted to us. And lead us not into temptation.'"

5 Then He said to them, "Suppose one of you has a friend, and goes to him at midnight and says to him, 'Friend, lend me three loaves;

6 for a friend of mine has come to me from a journey, and I have nothing to set before him';

7 and from inside he answers and says, 'Do not bother me; the door has already been shut and my children and I are in bed; I cannot get up and give you anything.'

8 "I tell you, even though he will not get up and give him anything because he is his friend, yet because of his persistence he will get up and give him as much as he needs.

9 "So I say to you, ask, and it will be given to you; seek, and you will find; knock, and it will be opened to you.

10 "For everyone who asks, receives; and he who seeks, finds; and to him who knocks, it will be opened.

11 "Now suppose one of you fathers is asked by his son for a fish;

he will not give him a snake instead of a fish, will he?

12 "Or if he is asked for an egg, he will not give him a scorpion, will he?

13 "If you then, being evil, know how to give good gifts to your children, how much more will your heavenly Father give the Holy Spirit to those who ask Him?"

14 And He was casting out a demon, and it was mute; when the demon had gone out, the mute man spoke; and the crowds were amazed.

15 But some of them said, "He casts out demons by Beelzebul, the ruler of the demons."

16 Others, to test Him, were demanding of Him a sign from heaven.

17 But He knew their thoughts and said to them, "Any kingdom divided against itself is laid waste; and a house divided against itself falls.

18 "If Satan also is divided against himself, how will his kingdom stand? For you say that I cast out demons by Beelzebul.

19 "And if I by Beelzebul cast out demons, by whom do your sons cast them out? So they will be your judges.

20 "But if I cast out demons by the finger of God, then the kingdom of God has come upon you.

21 "When a strong man, fully armed, guards his own house, his possessions are undisturbed.

22 "But when someone stronger than he attacks him and overpowers him, he takes away from him all his armor on which he had relied and distributes his plunder.

23 "He who is not with Me is against Me; and he who does not gather with Me, scatters.

24 "When the unclean spirit goes out of a man, it passes through waterless places seeking rest, and not finding any, it says, 'I will return to my house from which I came.'

25 "And when it comes, it finds it swept and put in order.

26 "Then it goes and takes along seven other spirits more evil than itself, and they go in and live there; and the last state of that man becomes worse than the first."

27 While Jesus was saying these things, one of the women in the crowd raised her voice and said to Him, "Blessed is the womb that bore You and the breasts at which You nursed."

28 But He said, "On the contrary, blessed are those who hear the word of God and observe it."

29 As the crowds were increasing, He began to say, "This generation is a wicked generation; it seeks for a sign, and yet no sign will be given to it but the sign of Jonah.

30 "For just as Jonah became a sign to the Ninevites, so will the Son of Man be to this generation.

31 "The Queen of the South will rise up with the men of this generation at the judgment and condemn them, because she came from the ends of the earth to hear the wisdom of Solomon; and behold, something greater than Solomon is here.

32 "The men of Nineveh will stand up with this generation at the judgment and condemn it, because they repented at the preaching of Jonah; and behold, something greater than Jonah is here.

33 "No one, after lighting a lamp, puts it away in a cellar nor under a basket, but on the lampstand, so that those who enter may see the light.

34 "The eye is the lamp of your body; when your eye is clear, your whole body also is full of light; but when it is bad, your body also is full of darkness.

35 "Then watch out that the light in you is not darkness.

36 "If therefore your whole body is full of light, with no dark part in it, it will be wholly illumined, as when the lamp illumines you with its rays."

37 Now when He had spoken, a Pharisee asked Him to have lunch with him; and He went in, and reclined at the table.

38 When the Pharisee saw it, he was surprised that He had not first ceremonially washed before the meal.

39 But the Lord said to him, "Now you Pharisees clean the outside of the cup and of the platter; but inside of you, you are full of robbery and wickedness.

40 "You foolish ones, did not He who made the outside make the inside also?

41 "But give that which is within as charity, and then all things are clean for you.

42 "But woe to you Pharisees! For you pay tithe of mint and rue and every kind of garden herb, and yet disregard justice and the love of God; but these are the things you should have done without neglecting the others.

43 "Woe to you Pharisees! For you love the chief seats in the synagogues and the respectful greetings in the market places.

44 "Woe to you! For you are like concealed tombs, and the people who walk over them are unaware of it."

45 One of the lawyers said to Him in reply, "Teacher, when You say this, You insult us too."

46 But He said, "Woe to you lawyers as well! For you weigh men down with burdens hard to bear, while you yourselves will not even touch the burdens with one of your fingers.

47 "Woe to you! For you build the tombs of the prophets, and it was your fathers who killed them.

48 "So you are witnesses and approve the deeds of your fathers; because it was they who killed them, and you build their tombs.

49 "For this reason also the wisdom of God said, 'I will send to them prophets and apostles, and some of them they will kill and some they will persecute,

50 so that the blood of all the prophets, shed since the foundation
of the world, may be charged against this generation,

51 from the blood of Abel to the blood of Zechariah, who was
killed between the altar and the house of God; yes, I tell you, it
shall be charged against this generation.'

52 "Woe to you lawyers! For you have taken away the key of
knowledge; you yourselves did not enter, and you hindered
those who were entering."

53 When He left there, the scribes and the Pharisees began to be
very hostile and to question Him closely on many subjects,

54 plotting against Him to catch Him in something He might say.

Matthew 6

1 "Beware of practicing your righteousness before men to be
noticed by them; otherwise you have no reward with your
Father who is in heaven.

2 "So when you give to the poor, do not sound a trumpet before
you, as the hypocrites do in the synagogues and in the streets,
so that they may be honored by men. Truly I say to you, they
have their reward in full.

3 "But when you give to the poor, do not let your left hand know
what your right hand is doing,

4 so that your giving will be in secret; and your Father who sees
what is done in secret will reward you.

5 "When you pray, you are not to be like the hypocrites; for they
love to stand and pray in the synagogues and on the street cor-
ners so that they may be seen by men. Truly I say to you, they
have their reward in full.

6 "But you, when you pray, go into your inner room, close your
door and pray to your Father who is in secret, and your Father
who sees what is done in secret will reward you.

7 "And when you are praying, do not use meaningless repetition as the Gentiles do, for they suppose that they will be heard for their many words.

8 "So do not be like them; for your Father knows what you need before you ask Him.

9 "Pray, then, in this way:
'Our Father who is in heaven,
Hallowed be Your name.

10 'Your kingdom come.
Your will be done,
On earth as it is in heaven.

11 'Give us this day our daily bread.

12 'And forgive us our debts, as we also have forgiven our debtors.

13 'And do not lead us into temptation, but deliver us from evil. [For Yours is the kingdom and the power and the glory forever. Amen.]'

14 "For if you forgive others for their transgressions, your heavenly Father will also forgive you.

15 "But if you do not forgive others, then your Father will not forgive your transgressions.

16 "Whenever you fast, do not put on a gloomy face as the hypocrites do, for they neglect their appearance so that they will be noticed by men when they are fasting. Truly I say to you, they have their reward in full.

17 "But you, when you fast, anoint your head and wash your face

18 so that your fasting will not be noticed by men, but by your Father who is in secret; and your Father who sees what is done in secret will reward you.

19 "Do not store up for yourselves treasures on earth, where moth and rust destroy, and where thieves break in and steal.

20 "But store up for yourselves treasures in heaven, where neither moth nor rust destroys, and where thieves do not break in or steal;

21 for where your treasure is, there your heart will be also.

22 "The eye is the lamp of the body; so then if your eye is clear, your whole body will be full of light.

23 "But if your eye is bad, your whole body will be full of darkness. If then the light that is in you is darkness, how great is the darkness!

24 "No one can serve two masters; for either he will hate the one and love the other, or he will be devoted to one and despise the other. You cannot serve God and wealth.

25 "For this reason I say to you, do not be worried about your life, as to what you will eat or what you will drink; nor for your body, as to what you will put on. Is not life more than food, and the body more than clothing?

26 "Look at the birds of the air, that they do not sow, nor reap nor gather into barns, and yet your heavenly Father feeds them. Are you not worth much more than they?

27 "And who of you by being worried can add a single hour to his life?

28 "And why are you worried about clothing? Observe how the lilies of the field grow; they do not toil nor do they spin,

29 yet I say to you that not even Solomon in all his glory clothed himself like one of these.

30 "But if God so clothes the grass of the field, which is alive today and tomorrow is thrown into the furnace, will He not much more clothe you? You of little faith!

31 "Do not worry then, saying, 'What will we eat?' or 'What will we drink?' or 'What will we wear for clothing?'

32 "For the Gentiles eagerly seek all these things; for your heavenly Father knows that you need all these things.

33 "But seek first His kingdom and His righteousness, and all these things will be added to you.

34 "So do not worry about tomorrow; for tomorrow will care for itself. Each day has enough trouble of its own.

2 Chronicles 20

1 Now it came about after this that the sons of Moab and the sons of Ammon, together with some of the Meunites, came to make war against Jehoshaphat.

2 Then some came and reported to Jehoshaphat, saying, "A great multitude is coming against you from beyond the sea, out of Aram and behold, they are in Hazazon-tamar (that is Engedi)."

3 Jehoshaphat was afraid and turned his attention to seek the LORD, and proclaimed a fast throughout all Judah.

4 So Judah gathered together to seek help from the LORD; they even came from all the cities of Judah to seek the LORD.

5 Then Jehoshaphat stood in the assembly of Judah and Jerusalem, in the house of the LORD before the new court,

6 and he said, "O LORD, the God of our fathers, are You not God in the heavens? And are You not ruler over all the kingdoms of the nations? Power and might are in Your hand so that no one can stand against You.

7 "Did You not, O our God, drive out the inhabitants of this land before Your people Israel and give it to the descendants of Abraham Your friend forever?

8 "They have lived in it, and have built You a sanctuary there for Your name, saying,

9 'Should evil come upon us, the sword, or judgment, or pestilence, or famine, we will stand before this house and before You (for Your name is in this house) and cry to You in our distress, and You will hear and deliver us.'

10 "Now behold, the sons of Ammon and Moab and Mount Seir, whom You did not let Israel invade when they came out of the land of Egypt (they turned aside from them and did not destroy them),

11 see how they are rewarding us by coming to drive us out from Your possession which You have given us as an inheritance.

12 "O our God, will You not judge them? For we are powerless before this great multitude who are coming against us; nor do we know what to do, but our eyes are on You."

13 All Judah was standing before the LORD, with their infants, their wives and their children.

14 Then in the midst of the assembly the Spirit of the LORD came upon Jahaziel the son of Zechariah, the son of Benaiah, the son of Jeiel, the son of Mattaniah, the Levite of the sons of Asaph;

15 and he said, "Listen, all Judah and the inhabitants of Jerusalem and King Jehoshaphat: thus says the LORD to you, 'Do not fear or be dismayed because of this great multitude, for the battle is not yours but God's.

16 'Tomorrow go down against them. Behold, they will come up by the ascent of Ziz, and you will find them at the end of the valley in front of the wilderness of Jeruel.

17 'You need not fight in this battle; station yourselves, stand and see the salvation of the LORD on your behalf, O Judah and Jerusalem.' Do not fear or be dismayed; tomorrow go out to face them, for the LORD is with you."

18 Jehoshaphat bowed his head with his face to the ground, and all Judah and the inhabitants of Jerusalem fell down before the LORD, worshiping the LORD.

19 The Levites, from the sons of the Kohathites and of the sons of the Korahites, stood up to praise the LORD God of Israel, with a very loud voice.

20 They rose early in the morning and went out to the wilderness of Tekoa; and when they went out, Jehoshaphat stood and said, "Listen to me, O Judah and inhabitants of Jerusalem, put your trust in the LORD your God and you will be established. Put your trust in His prophets and succeed."

21 When he had consulted with the people, he appointed those who sang to the LORD and those who praised Him in holy attire, as they went out before the army and said, "Give thanks to the LORD, for His lovingkindness is everlasting."

22 When they began singing and praising, the LORD set ambushes against the sons of Ammon, Moab and Mount Seir, who had come against Judah; so they were routed.

23 For the sons of Ammon and Moab rose up against the inhabitants of Mount Seir destroying them completely; and when they had finished with the inhabitants of Seir, they helped to destroy one another.

24 When Judah came to the lookout of the wilderness, they looked toward the multitude, and behold, they were corpses lying on the ground, and no one had escaped.

25 When Jehoshaphat and his people came to take their spoil, they found much among them, including goods, garments and valuable things which they took for themselves, more than they could carry. And they were three days taking the spoil because there was so much.

26 Then on the fourth day they assembled in the valley of Beracah, for there they blessed the LORD. Therefore they have named that place "The Valley of Beracah" until today.

27 Every man of Judah and Jerusalem returned with Jehoshaphat at their head, returning to Jerusalem with joy, for the LORD had made them to rejoice over their enemies.

28 They came to Jerusalem with harps, lyres and trumpets to the house of the LORD.

29 And the dread of God was on all the kingdoms of the lands when they heard that the LORD had fought against the enemies of Israel.

30 So the kingdom of Jehoshaphat was at peace, for his God gave him rest on all sides.

31 Now Jehoshaphat reigned over Judah. He was thirty-five years old when he became king, and he reigned in Jerusalem twenty-five years. And his mother's name was Azubah the daughter of Shilhi.

32 He walked in the way of his father Asa and did not depart from it, doing right in the sight of the LORD.

33 The high places, however, were not removed; the people had not yet directed their hearts to the God of their fathers.

34 Now the rest of the acts of Jehoshaphat, first to last, behold, they are written in the annals of Jehu the son of Hanani, which is recorded in the Book of the Kings of Israel.

35 After this Jehoshaphat king of Judah allied himself with Ahaziah king of Israel. He acted wickedly in so doing.

36 So he allied himself with him to make ships to go to Tarshish, and they made the ships in Ezion-geber.

37 Then Eliezer the son of Dodavahu of Mareshah prophesied against Jehoshaphat saying, "Because you have allied yourself with Ahaziah, the LORD has destroyed your works." So the ships were broken and could not go to Tarshish.

Isaiah 36

1 Now in the fourteenth year of King Hezekiah, Sennacherib king of Assyria came up against all the fortified cities of Judah and seized them.

2 And the king of Assyria sent Rabshakeh from Lachish to Jerusalem to King Hezekiah with a large army. And he stood by the conduit of the upper pool on the highway of the fuller's field.

3 Then Eliakim the son of Hilkiah, who was over the household, and Shebna the scribe, and Joah the son of Asaph, the recorder, came out to him.

4 Then Rabshakeh said to them, "Say now to Hezekiah, 'Thus says the great king, the king of Assyria, "What is this confidence that you have?

5 "I say, 'Your counsel and strength for the war are only empty words.' Now on whom do you rely, that you have rebelled against me?

6 "Behold, you rely on the staff of this crushed reed, even on Egypt, on which if a man leans, it will go into his hand and pierce it. So is Pharaoh king of Egypt to all who rely on him.

7 "But if you say to me, 'We trust in the LORD our God,' is it not He whose high places and whose altars Hezekiah has taken away and has said to Judah and to Jerusalem, 'You shall worship before this altar'?

8 "Now therefore, come make a bargain with my master the king of Assyria, and I will give you two thousand horses, if you are able on your part to set riders on them.

9 "How then can you repulse one official of the least of my master's servants and rely on Egypt for chariots and for horsemen?

10 "Have I now come up without the LORD's approval against this land to destroy it? The LORD said to me, 'Go up against this land and destroy it.'"

11 Then Eliakim and Shebna and Joah said to Rabshakeh, "Speak now to your servants in Aramaic, for we understand it; and do not speak with us in Judean in the hearing of the people who are on the wall."

12 But Rabshakeh said, "Has my master sent me only to your master and to you to speak these words, and not to the men who sit on the wall, doomed to eat their own dung and drink their own urine with you?"

13 Then Rabshakeh stood and cried with a loud voice in Judean and said, "Hear the words of the great king, the king of Assyria.

14 "Thus says the king, 'Do not let Hezekiah deceive you, for he will not be able to deliver you;

15 nor let Hezekiah make you trust in the LORD, saying, "The LORD will surely deliver us, this city will not be given into the hand of the king of Assyria."

16 'Do not listen to Hezekiah,' for thus says the king of Assyria, 'Make your peace with me and come out to me, and eat each of his vine and each of his fig tree and drink each of the waters of his own cistern,

17 until I come and take you away to a land like your own land, a land of grain and new wine, a land of bread and vineyards.

18 'Beware that Hezekiah does not mislead you, saying, "The LORD will deliver us." Has any one of the gods of the nations delivered his land from the hand of the king of Assyria?

19 'Where are the gods of Hamath and Arpad? Where are the gods of Sepharvaim? And when have they delivered Samaria from my hand?

20 'Who among all the gods of these lands have delivered their land from my hand, that the LORD would deliver Jerusalem from my hand?'"

21 But they were silent and answered him not a word; for the king's commandment was, "Do not answer him."

22 Then Eliakim the son of Hilkiah, who was over the household, and Shebna the scribe and Joah the son of Asaph, the recorder,

came to Hezekiah with their clothes torn and told him the
words of Rabshakeh.

Isaiah 37

1 And when King Hezekiah heard it, he tore his clothes, covered
himself with sackcloth and entered the house of the LORD.

2 Then he sent Eliakim who was over the household with Shebna
the scribe and the elders of the priests, covered with sackcloth,
to Isaiah the prophet, the son of Amoz.

3 They said to him, "Thus says Hezekiah, 'This day is a day of
distress, rebuke and rejection; for children have come to birth,
and there is no strength to deliver.

4 'Perhaps the LORD your God will hear the words of Rabshakeh,
whom his master the king of Assyria has sent to reproach the
living God, and will rebuke the words which the LORD your
God has heard. Therefore, offer a prayer for the remnant that is
left.'"

5 So the servants of King Hezekiah came to Isaiah.

6 Isaiah said to them, "Thus you shall say to your master, 'Thus
says the LORD, "Do not be afraid because of the words that you
have heard, with which the servants of the king of Assyria have
blasphemed Me.

7 "Behold, I will put a spirit in him so that he will hear a rumor
and return to his own land. And I will make him fall by the
sword in his own land."'"

8 Then Rabshakeh returned and found the king of Assyria fighting
against Libnah, for he had heard that the king had left Lachish.

9 When he heard them say concerning Tirhakah king of Cush,
"He has come out to fight against you," and when he heard it
he sent messengers to Hezekiah, saying,

10 "Thus you shall say to Hezekiah king of Judah, 'Do not let your God in whom you trust deceive you, saying, "Jerusalem will not be given into the hand of the king of Assyria."

11 'Behold, you have heard what the kings of Assyria have done to all the lands, destroying them completely. So will you be spared?

12 'Did the gods of those nations which my fathers have destroyed deliver them, even Gozan and Haran and Rezeph and the sons of Eden who were in Telassar?

13 'Where is the king of Hamath, the king of Arpad, the king of the city of Sepharvaim, and of Hena and Ivvah?'"

14 Then Hezekiah took the letter from the hand of the messengers and read it, and he went up to the house of the LORD and spread it out before the LORD.

15 Hezekiah prayed to the LORD saying,

16 "O LORD of hosts, the God of Israel, who is enthroned above the cherubim, You are the God, You alone, of all the kingdoms of the earth. You have made heaven and earth.

17 "Incline Your ear, O LORD, and hear; open Your eyes, O LORD, and see; and listen to all the words of Sennacherib, who sent them to reproach the living God.

18 "Truly, O LORD, the kings of Assyria have devastated all the countries and their lands,

19 and have cast their gods into the fire, for they were not gods but the work of men's hands, wood and stone. So they have destroyed them.

20 "Now, O LORD our God, deliver us from his hand that all the kingdoms of the earth may know that You alone, LORD, are God."

21 Then Isaiah the son of Amoz sent word to Hezekiah, saying, "Thus says the LORD, the God of Israel, 'Because you have prayed to Me about Sennacherib king of Assyria,

22 this is the word that the Lord has spoken against him: "She has despised you and mocked you, the virgin daughter of Zion; she has shaken her head behind you, the daughter of Jerusalem!

23 "Whom have you reproached and blasphemed? And against whom have you raised your voice and haughtily lifted up your eyes? Against the Holy One of Israel!

24 "Through your servants you have reproached the LORD, and you have said, 'With my many chariots I came up to the heights of the mountains, to the remotest parts of Lebanon; and I cut down its tall cedars and its choice cypresses. And I will go to its highest peak, its thickest forest.

25 'I dug wells and drank waters, and with the sole of my feet I dried up all the rivers of Egypt.'

26 "Have you not heard? Long ago I did it, from ancient times I planned it. Now I have brought it to pass, that you should turn fortified cities into ruinous heaps.

27 "Therefore their inhabitants were short of strength, they were dismayed and put to shame; they were as the vegetation of the field and as the green herb, as grass on the housetops is scorched before it is grown up.

28 "But I know your sitting down and your going out and your coming in and your raging against Me.

29 "Because of your raging against Me and because your arrogance has come up to My ears, therefore I will put My hook in your nose, and My bridle in your lips, and I will turn you back by the way which you came.

30 "Then this shall be the sign for you: you will eat this year what grows of itself, in the second year what springs from the same, and in the third year sow, reap, plant vineyards and eat their fruit.

31 "The surviving remnant of the house of Judah will again take root downward and bear fruit upward.

32 "For out of Jerusalem will go forth a remnant and out of Mount Zion survivors. The zeal of the LORD of hosts will perform this."'

33 "Therefore, thus says the LORD concerning the king of Assyria, 'He will not come to this city or shoot an arrow there; and he will not come before it with a shield, or throw up a siege ramp against it.

34 'By the way that he came, by the same he will return, and he will not come to this city,' declares the LORD.

35 'For I will defend this city to save it for My own sake and for My servant David's sake.'"

36 Then the angel of the LORD went out and struck 185,000 in the camp of the Assyrians; and when men arose early in the morning, behold, all of these were dead.

37 So Sennacherib king of Assyria departed and returned home and lived at Nineveh.

38 It came about as he was worshiping in the house of Nisroch his god, that Adrammelech and Sharezer his sons killed him with the sword; and they escaped into the land of Ararat. And Esarhaddon his son became king in his place.

John 3

1 Now there was a man of the Pharisees, named Nicodemus, a ruler of the Jews;

2 this man came to Jesus by night and said to Him, "Rabbi, we know that You have come from God as a teacher; for no one can do these signs that You do unless God is with him."

3 Jesus answered and said to him, "Truly, truly, I say to you, unless one is born again he cannot see the kingdom of God."

4 Nicodemus said to Him, "How can a man be born when he is old? He cannot enter a second time into his mother's womb and be born, can he?"

5 Jesus answered, "Truly, truly, I say to you, unless one is born of water and the Spirit he cannot enter into the kingdom of God.

6 "That which is born of the flesh is flesh, and that which is born of the Spirit is spirit.

7 "Do not be amazed that I said to you, 'You must be born again.'

8 "The wind blows where it wishes and you hear the sound of it, but do not know where it comes from and where it is going; so is everyone who is born of the Spirit."

9 Nicodemus said to Him, "How can these things be?"

10 Jesus answered and said to him, "Are you the teacher of Israel and do not understand these things?

11 "Truly, truly, I say to you, we speak of what we know and testify of what we have seen, and you do not accept our testimony.

12 "If I told you earthly things and you do not believe, how will you believe if I tell you heavenly things?

13 "No one has ascended into heaven, but He who descended from heaven: the Son of Man.

14 "As Moses lifted up the serpent in the wilderness, even so must the Son of Man be lifted up;

15 "so that whoever believes will in Him have eternal life.

16 "For God so loved the world, that He gave His only begotten Son, that whoever believes in Him shall not perish, but have eternal life.

17 "For God did not send the Son into the world to judge the world, but that the world might be saved through Him.

18 "He who believes in Him is not judged; he who does not believe has been judged already, because he has not believed in the name of the only begotten Son of God.

19 "This is the judgment, that the Light has come into the world, and men loved the darkness rather than the Light, for their deeds were evil.

20 "For everyone who does evil hates the Light, and does not come to the Light for fear that his deeds will be exposed.

21 "But he who practices the truth comes to the Light, so that his deeds may be manifested as having been wrought in God."

22 After these things Jesus and His disciples came into the land of Judea, and there He was spending time with them and baptizing.

23 John also was baptizing in Aenon near Salim, because there was much water there; and people were coming and were being baptized—

24 for John had not yet been thrown into prison.

25 Therefore there arose a discussion on the part of John's disciples with a Jew about purification.

26 And they came to John and said to him, "Rabbi, He who was with you beyond the Jordan, to whom you have testified, behold, He is baptizing and all are coming to Him."

27 John answered and said, "A man can receive nothing unless it has been given him from heaven.

28 "You yourselves are my witnesses that I said, 'I am not the Christ,' but, 'I have been sent ahead of Him.'

29 "He who has the bride is the bridegroom; but the friend of the bridegroom, who stands and hears him, rejoices greatly because of the bridegroom's voice. So this joy of mine has been made full.

30 "He must increase, but I must decrease.

31 "He who comes from above is above all, he who is of the earth is from the earth and speaks of the earth. He who comes from heaven is above all.

32 "What He has seen and heard, of that He testifies; and no one receives His testimony.

33 "He who has received His testimony has set his seal to this, that God is true.

34 "For He whom God has sent speaks the words of God; for He gives the Spirit without measure.

35 "The Father loves the Son and has given all things into His hand.

36 "He who believes in the Son has eternal life; but he who does not obey the Son will not see life, but the wrath of God abides on him."

Matthew 18

1 At that time the disciples came to Jesus and said, "Who then is greatest in the kingdom of heaven?"

2 And He called a child to Himself and set him before them,

3 and said, "Truly I say to you, unless you are converted and become like children, you will not enter the kingdom of heaven.

4 "Whoever then humbles himself as this child, he is the greatest in the kingdom of heaven.

5 "And whoever receives one such child in My name receives Me;

6 "but whoever causes one of these little ones who believe in Me to stumble, it would be better for him to have a heavy millstone hung around his neck, and to be drowned in the depth of the sea.

7 "Woe to the world because of its stumbling blocks! For it is inevitable that stumbling blocks come; but woe to that man through whom the stumbling block comes!

8 "If your hand or your foot causes you to stumble, cut it off and throw it from you; it is better for you to enter life crippled or lame, than to have two hands or two feet and be cast into the eternal fire.

9 "If your eye causes you to stumble, pluck it out and throw it from you. It is better for you to enter life with one eye, than to have two eyes and be cast into the fiery hell.

10 "See that you do not despise one of these little ones, for I say to you that their angels in heaven continually see the face of My Father who is in heaven.

11 ["For the Son of Man has come to save that which was lost.]

12 "What do you think? If any man has a hundred sheep, and one of them has gone astray, does he not leave the ninety-nine on the mountains and go and search for the one that is straying?

13 "If it turns out that he finds it, truly I say to you, he rejoices over it more than over the ninety-nine which have not gone astray.

14 "So it is not the will of your Father who is in heaven that one of these little ones perish.

15 "If your brother sins, go and show him his fault in private; if he listens to you, you have won your brother.

16 "But if he does not listen to you, take one or two more with you, so that BY THE MOUTH OF TWO OR THREE WITNESSES EVERY FACT MAY BE CONFIRMED.

17 "If he refuses to listen to them, tell it to the church; and if he refuses to listen even to the church, let him be to you as a Gentile and a tax collector.

18 "Truly I say to you, whatever you bind on earth shall have been bound in heaven; and whatever you loose on earth shall have been loosed in heaven.

19 "Again I say to you, that if two of you agree on earth about anything that they may ask, it shall be done for them by My Father who is in heaven.

20 "For where two or three have gathered together in My name, I am there in their midst."

21 Then Peter came and said to Him, "Lord, how often shall my brother sin against me and I forgive him? Up to seven times?"

22 Jesus said to him, "I do not say to you, up to seven times, but up to seventy times seven.

23 "For this reason the kingdom of heaven may be compared to a king who wished to settle accounts with his slaves.

24 "When he had begun to settle them, one who owed him ten thousand talents was brought to him.

25 "But since he did not have the means to repay, his lord commanded him to be sold, along with his wife and children and all that he had, and repayment to be made.

26 "So the slave fell to the ground and prostrated himself before him, saying, 'Have patience with me and I will repay you everything.'

27 "And the lord of that slave felt compassion and released him and forgave him the debt.

28 "But that slave went out and found one of his fellow slaves who owed him a hundred denarii; and he seized him and began to choke him, saying, 'Pay back what you owe.'

29 "So his fellow slave fell to the ground and began to plead with him, saying, 'Have patience with me and I will repay you.'

30 "But he was unwilling and went and threw him in prison until he should pay back what was owed.

31 "So when his fellow slaves saw what had happened, they were deeply grieved and came and reported to their lord all that had happened.

32 "Then summoning him, his lord said to him, 'You wicked slave, I forgave you all that debt because you pleaded with me.

33 'Should you not also have had mercy on your fellow slave, in the same way that I had mercy on you?'

34 "And his lord, moved with anger, handed him over to the torturers until he should repay all that was owed him.

35 "My heavenly Father will also do the same to you, if each of
you does not forgive his brother from your heart."

Matthew 26

1 When Jesus had finished all these words, He said to His disciples,

2 "You know that after two days the Passover is coming, and the
Son of Man is to be handed over for crucifixion."

3 Then the chief priests and the elders of the people were gathered together in the court of the high priest, named Caiaphas;

4 and they plotted together to seize Jesus by stealth and kill Him.

5 But they were saying, "Not during the festival, otherwise a riot
might occur among the people."

6 Now when Jesus was in Bethany, at the home of Simon the
leper,

7 a woman came to Him with an alabaster vial of very costly perfume, and she poured it on His head as He reclined at the table.

8 But the disciples were indignant when they saw this, and said,
"Why this waste?

9 "For this perfume might have been sold for a high price and the
money given to the poor."

10 But Jesus, aware of this, said to them, "Why do you bother the
woman? For she has done a good deed to Me.

11 "For you always have the poor with you; but you do not always
have Me.

12 "For when she poured this perfume on My body, she did it to
prepare Me for burial.

13 "Truly I say to you, wherever this gospel is preached in the whole world, what this woman has done will also be spoken of in memory of her."

14 Then one of the twelve, named Judas Iscariot, went to the chief priests

15 and said, "What are you willing to give me to betray Him to you?" And they weighed out thirty pieces of silver to him.

16 From then on he began looking for a good opportunity to betray Jesus.

17 Now on the first day of Unleavened Bread the disciples came to Jesus and asked, "Where do You want us to prepare for You to eat the Passover?"

18 And He said, "Go into the city to a certain man, and say to him, 'The Teacher says, "My time is near; I am to keep the Passover at your house with My disciples."'"

19 The disciples did as Jesus had directed them; and they prepared the Passover.

20 Now when evening came, Jesus was reclining at the table with the twelve disciples.

21 As they were eating, He said, "Truly I say to you that one of you will betray Me."

22 Being deeply grieved, they each one began to say to Him, "Surely not I, Lord?"

23 And He answered, "He who dipped his hand with Me in the bowl is the one who will betray Me.

24 "The Son of Man is to go, just as it is written of Him; but woe to that man by whom the Son of Man is betrayed! It would have been good for that man if he had not been born."

25 And Judas, who was betraying Him, said, "Surely it is not I, Rabbi?" Jesus said to him, "You have said it yourself."

26 While they were eating, Jesus took some bread, and after a blessing, He broke it and gave it to the disciples, and said, "Take, eat; this is My body."

27 And when He had taken a cup and given thanks, He gave it to them, saying, "Drink from it, all of you;

28 "for this is My blood of the covenant, which is poured out for many for forgiveness of sins.

29 "But I say to you, I will not drink of this fruit of the vine from now on until that day when I drink it new with you in My Father's kingdom."

30 After singing a hymn, they went out to the Mount of Olives.

31 Then Jesus said to them, "You will all fall away because of Me this night, for it is written, 'I WILL STRIKE DOWN THE SHEPHERD, AND THE SHEEP OF THE FLOCK SHALL BE SCATTERED.'

32 "But after I have been raised, I will go ahead of you to Galilee."

33 But Peter said to Him, "Even though all may fall away because of You, I will never fall away."

34 Jesus said to him, "Truly I say to you that this very night, before a rooster crows, you will deny Me three times."

35 Peter said to Him, "Even if I have to die with You, I will not deny You." All the disciples said the same thing too.

36 Then Jesus came with them to a place called Gethsemane, and said to His disciples, "Sit here while I go over there and pray."

37 And He took with Him Peter and the two sons of Zebedee, and began to be grieved and distressed.

38 Then He said to them, "My soul is deeply grieved, to the point of death; remain here and keep watch with Me."

39 And He went a little beyond them, and fell on His face and prayed, saying, "My Father, if it is possible, let this cup pass from Me; yet not as I will, but as You will."

40 And He came to the disciples and found them sleeping, and said to Peter, "So, you men could not keep watch with Me for one hour?

41 "Keep watching and praying that you may not enter into temptation; the spirit is willing, but the flesh is weak."

42 He went away again a second time and prayed, saying, "My Father, if this cannot pass away unless I drink it, Your will be done."

43 Again He came and found them sleeping, for their eyes were heavy.

44 And He left them again, and went away and prayed a third time, saying the same thing once more.

45 Then He came to the disciples and said to them, "Are you still sleeping and resting? Behold, the hour is at hand and the Son of Man is being betrayed into the hands of sinners.

46 "Get up, let us be going; behold, the one who betrays Me is at hand!"

47 While He was still speaking, behold, Judas, one of the twelve, came up accompanied by a large crowd with swords and clubs, who came from the chief priests and elders of the people.

48 Now he who was betraying Him gave them a sign, saying, "Whomever I kiss, He is the one; seize Him."

49 Immediately Judas went to Jesus and said, "Hail, Rabbi!" and kissed Him.

50 And Jesus said to him, "Friend, do what you have come for." Then they came and laid hands on Jesus and seized Him.

51 And behold, one of those who were with Jesus reached and drew out his sword, and struck the slave of the high priest and cut off his ear.

52 Then Jesus said to him, "Put your sword back into its place; for all those who take up the sword shall perish by the sword.

53 "Or do you think that I cannot appeal to My Father, and He will at once put at My disposal more than twelve legions of angels?

54 "How then will the Scriptures be fulfilled, which say that it must happen this way?"

55 At that time Jesus said to the crowds, "Have you come out with swords and clubs to arrest Me as you would against a robber? Every day I used to sit in the temple teaching and you did not seize Me.

56 "But all this has taken place to fulfill the Scriptures of the prophets." Then all the disciples left Him and fled.

57 Those who had seized Jesus led Him away to Caiaphas, the high priest, where the scribes and the elders were gathered together.

58 But Peter was following Him at a distance as far as the courtyard of the high priest, and entered in, and sat down with the officers to see the outcome.

59 Now the chief priests and the whole Council kept trying to obtain false testimony against Jesus, so that they might put Him to death.

60 They did not find any, even though many false witnesses came forward. But later on two came forward,

61 and said, "This man stated, 'I am able to destroy the temple of God and to rebuild it in three days.'"

62 The high priest stood up and said to Him, "Do You not answer? What is it that these men are testifying against You?"

63 But Jesus kept silent. And the high priest said to Him, "I adjure You by the living God, that You tell us whether You are the Christ, the Son of God."

64 Jesus said to him, "You have said it yourself; nevertheless I tell you, hereafter you will see THE SON OF MAN SITTING AT THE RIGHT HAND OF POWER, AND COMING ON THE CLOUDS OF HEAVEN."

65 Then the high priest tore his robes and said, "He has blasphemed! What further need do we have of witnesses? Behold, you have now heard the blasphemy;

66 what do you think?" They answered, "He deserves death!"

67 Then they spat in His face and beat Him with their fists; and others slapped Him,

68 and said, "Prophesy to us, You Christ; who is the one who hit You?"

69 Now Peter was sitting outside in the courtyard, and a servant-girl came to him and said, "You too were with Jesus the Galilean."

70 But he denied it before them all, saying, "I do not know what you are talking about."

71 When he had gone out to the gateway, another servant-girl saw him and said to those who were there, "This man was with Jesus of Nazareth."

72 And again he denied it with an oath, "I do not know the man."

73 A little later the bystanders came up and said to Peter, "Surely you too are one of them; for even the way you talk gives you away."

74 Then he began to curse and swear, "I do not know the man!" And immediately a rooster crowed.

75 And Peter remembered the word which Jesus had said, "Before a rooster crows, you will deny Me three times." And he went out and wept bitterly.